THE MOVABLE NEST:

A MOTHER/DAUGHTER COMPANION

THE MOVABLE NEST:

A MOTHER/DAUGHTER COMPANION

EDITORS:
MARILYN KALLET &
KATHRYN STRIPLING BYER

HELICON NINE EDITIONS
KANSAS CITY & LOS ANGELES

Book design by Tim Barnhart.
Cover art: Suzanne Stryk. *Little Wing*, 2005.

Helicon Nine Editions, a non-profit small press, is funded in part by
the Miller-Mellor Association, the N.W. Dible Foundation, the
National Endowment for the Arts, a federal agency,
the Kansas Arts Commission and the Missouri Arts Council, state agencies.

LIBRARY OF CONGRESS CATALOGING-IN-PUBLICATION DATA

The movable nest : a mother/daughter companion / editors, Marilyn Kallet &
Kathryn Stripling Byer.
    p. cm.
Includes index.
An anthology of nonfiction essays, poetry, stories, and letters, focusing on
mothers and college-age daughters saying goodbye to one another.
ISBN-13: 978-1-884235-39-9 (pbk. : alk. paper)
1. Mothers and daughters--Literary collections. 2. Separation (Psychology)--
Literary collections. 3. Farewells--Literary collections. 4. Empty nesters--
Literary collections. 5. American literature--Women authors. 6. American lit-
erature--21st century. I. Kallet, Marilyn, 1946- II. Byer, Kathryn Stripling.
PS509.M6M73 2007
810.8'035252--dc22

                                                    2007039827

Manufactured in the United States of America
FIRST EDITION
HELICON NINE EDITIONS
KANSAS CITY AND LOS ANGELES

for Heather Miriam Gross
and Corinna Lynnette Byer

Marilyn Kallet with her daughter, Heather Miriam Gross.

CONTENTS

INTRODUCTION

Five years ago, I began to complain to Kathryn Stripling Byer about my sixteen-year-old daughter's desire to leave home for music school. Heather and I had just returned from campus visits, and my mood vacillated between astonished pride and dread. My percussionist daughter was going to fly the coop, two years early, to boot. Kay responded with intelligent sympathy. Her daughter Cory was then an undergraduate at the University of Chicago. Cory had left the green slopes of North Carolina for the snowy windy land of Chicago—to hear Kay tell it, the weather was part of the insult to a mother's heart. Chicago might as well have been the moon.

Kay and I began to talk about how useful it might be to compose an anthology on "leaving the nest." Perhaps the act of compiling such a book would help us to stay sane. For me, Kay's eloquent poems on the subject were the clincher. In addition to her essay, "Last Day," her poetry also sings the complexities of leave-taking.

Writer-mothers use their art both as a way of recording their daughters' departures, and of restoring balance. But what kind of metaphors and which myths do women writers draw upon to help them through such difficult transitions? My hypothesis was that most of our writers would not find the image of an "empty nest" very engaging.

In her essay for this volume, Pat Mora plays with the idea of the "movable nest," a dynamic and artistic point of reference. In gathering selections for our book, I had hoped that I would find such models, women who would help me to grapple with my situation through their artistic ways of coping with loss. Nothing in my experience corresponded to "emptiness" during our preparations for Heather's leaving for the North Carolina School of the Arts. There were no obvious cultural guidelines, no Hallmark greeting-card section on the subject of letting go of a daughter (though there is one on the loss of a pet).

In gathering the material for this anthology, we chose selections that are imaginative, gutsy, and often lyrical. The first section, "Call Me, Even if You're Happy," includes poems, stories, essays and a journal that recount the difficult task of bidding farewell to our daughters, seeing them off into their own lives. Against clichés, a few of the mothers tell us that they felt some relief when their daughters left home. There's an admirable lack of sentimentality in Sarah Gorham's sketches, "A Woman Drawn Twice." Alice Friman's "Letting Go" sets a fierce, honest tone, conveying her sense of accomplishment in raising a capable daughter. Here Alice meditates both on caring for her aging mother and on how she felt when her talented daughter Lillian left home. She compares the temporary emptiness a mother might feel when a daughter leaves for college with that of postpartum blues. Emptiness does not prevail: "To have my daughter who had been through so much walk out that door with the confidence and the wholeness it would take to grab onto experience and weave into the fabric of a life—*her* life—was a joy indeed."

To dramatize the depths of their feelings, some authors chose the myth of Demeter and Persephone to speak of loss and love. Myth widened and deepened the field of goodbyes, lifting it from the private realm and reminding us of rituals of return. For poets Rita Dove and Rebecca McClanahan, myth offered ancient masks to wear for this age-old drama of separation and reunion.

In several instances, the ready-for-flight daughters, or those who had long ago left the nest, composed selections for our anthology to accompany the writings of their mothers. Libby Martinez's personal essay "Coming Home" adds resonance to Pat Mora's "The Movable Nest." Photographer Lillian Wilson, daughter of Alice Friman, composed "Leaving Mother" to compliment her mother's "Letting Go." And Corinna Scott Byer's poem reveals the same love of place and family that permeates the work of her mother, Kathryn Stripling Byer. Does it surprise us that the daughters of creative women have their own songs, their stories to tell?

We received breakthrough writings on themes pertaining to

adoption. Meg Kearney's essay provides us with the title for our second section, "Hello, Mother, Goodbye." Meg's essay explores the yearning and loss that she experienced in the search for her birthmother. Colette Inez's poetry sings about these themes as well, adding honest anger and prophetic self-definition to the mix. In "Tell Her, Then Go," Pamela Schoenewaldt's narrator speaks from the point of view of the adoptive mother, in a poignant story about exorcising the birthmother from her kitchen.

Rather than bidding farewell to daughters, several of our authors chose to write about saying goodbye to their own mothers. These selections, gathered in section two, offer tender reflections on leaving home, as well as stories about caring for aging mothers, about grieving and healing.

Letting go of our daughters is an ongoing challenge. They leave us and return, to take off again. Each goodbye is wrenching. Yet we take pride in having raised young women who can fend for themselves with creativity. After they leave us, we learn to take back our own lives. For me, the hardest part was preparing for Heather's departure. Once she had made the adjustment to boarding school, so did I. My writing was waiting for me when the house grew quiet.

For us mothers, the "returns" are all the more lovely, as our daughters come home to us with new poise and new perspectives on home. As we mature, we return to our mothers in memory, with movements toward reconciliation in our words. The selections in our anthology are permeated with the theme of "return." Persephone and Demeter lived the tale, as do the mothers who open the extension on the dining-room table to prepare for Thanksgiving, the daughters who plant flowers on the graves, the grandmothers, keepers of the old stories, who lean forward to remember, the granddaughters who listen and record.

What we did not anticipate when we began our collection of creative leave-takings was how much joy we would find in these selections. When our daughters come home again we learn to know them as adults, as the companions we knew they could become. My daughter will be twenty-two this summer. She's poised, intelligent, finishing her music degree at Northwestern, ready to enter the graduate program in Journalism at Medill. Once in a while she calls in a younger voice, asking for "motherly advice." Not long ago, she phoned to complain about a sadistic visiting conductor. I asked if she would like me to send her a chocolate voodoo doll to help with her anger. Our call ended with peals of laughter. The doll I sent her was made of good dark chocolate, of course!

The cell phone has revolutionized our relationships with our daughters. True, they still expect us to be on call, and to be an extension of them. Sometimes it seems that we have given birth to our mothers! But the phone calls permit us to hear that they are safe and happy, to detect notes of danger, to provide the words of comfort they still need—will always need—from their mothers.

Marilyn Kallet

I. Call Me, Even If You're Happy

PAT MORA

The Movable Nest

"How's my first baby?" asks Mom, referring to me as I approach sixty. The nest I return to weekly is my mother's voice on the phone. Even now, when she lives with only the occasional long- or short-term memory drifting through, her voice is strong and witty.

"I think I look darn good for eighty-five. Don't you, Pat dear?" she laughs. Her voice, its timbre and modulations, is a safe place she created from the moment when, a young and inexperienced mother, she held me and talked softly to me at the hospital in El Paso, Texas. I was going to say "the first time she talked to me," but I imagine through my first months she patted her abdomen and spoke to me inside.

What does it feel like, this family nest? Twigs, a bed, a sofa, a lap, a hug? In the poem "It Might Be Dangerous," I wrote, "I'm the middle woman, / not my mother, not my daughter." I study the small black-and-white picture of Mom expecting me. Life's mystery. At a recent writing conference, students in their twenties reacted negatively to the word *womb* in one of the family stories we were discussing. "It's constricting," they said, some with a shudder. Maybe the difference is age or exhaustion, but imagining my mini-self floating along for a spell in my mother's womb, my flesh boat, sounds delightful, a deep dream, hearing her voice in English and Spanish, unseen and carefree hearing her laugh, accompanying her, mulling about my next project effortlessly. Such riding sounds like a good morning of preparing for writing. Incubation.

> Some women hold me when I need to dream,
> Rock, rocked, my first red anger through the night.
> —*Communion*

Mother's voice returns me to the rock house where my three

1

siblings and I grew up. In my parents' bedroom, I see the large framed image of Our Lady of Guadalupe. Do her bare feet feel the arc, the crescent moon, on which she stands or floats or rides? A comforting notion, standing on a cosmic cupped hand, an open object that floats and rocks and in which a person could also curl and rest or drift to sleep, to dream, a bed in the universe, a celestial boat, a heavenly grin.

Mother, like all great teachers, breathed her strong and independent spirit into me, letting me witness her daily solutions whether in the kitchen or on the page and yet sustaining me in my explorations.

"I could never bake that cake, dear."

"What a good idea you had for ending that speech."

Mom didn't restrain me from exploring the world; the non-traveler never asked her daughter to forego trips to Pakistan or China; defying stereotypes, my Latina mother didn't and doesn't use guilt as a chain. She gave me the benefit of what she'd learned and wanted me to exceed her as I want my two daughters to exceed me, to learn from my mistakes, to go where I didn't or couldn't.

"This is the last law test, Libby. You can make it!"

"This is the last week of vet school, Cissy. Shall I put on my short cheerleader outfit again? I was going to put it up in moth balls."

I remember sitting in some boring summer college classes after I was married and writing my parents long letters knowing that what I wrote about the garden my husband and I were planting, the recipes I was trying, or what I'd be teaching in the fall—my words—mattered to them. They had moved to Santa Monica where Mother still lives her now restricted life. Although I'm sure I was sad when they sold the rock home in which my three siblings and I had grown up, I never felt the nest, the secure place where I found balance, had disappeared. I savor the intimate sound, song syllables, of the word for nest in Spanish, *nido*, and feel enmeshment, bodies and lives safely entangled. Like my daughter, Libby,

I imagine psychologists frowning and dialing for the astute assistance of psychiatrists, psychologists with little knowledge or interest in the sustaining closeness of Latino families perhaps.

While I ponder the image of the Virgin floating on an arc, I decide to wash the dishes, and the phone rings. A friend says she wants to drop by an article she wrote on Our Lady of Guadalupe. My heart-self pokes my skeptical self. Synchronicity.

Noah built his ark to save his family and earth's creatures from the deluge. I play with the notion of a female arc, the arc of our story, the curve of our arms when we hug, and I imagine tipping that final letter c up to form a cup, a drifting comforting shell, also a life-saver, woven of family stories, voice scraps, long gray hairs, recipes, streams of advice, phone wires, e-mails, and satellite signals. A sustaining curved vessel, its rhythm is familiar, like Mom's voice and the voices of grandmothers and aunts, waiting there when I need them. And need them I will, and my daughters will, for life can be hard and lonely as a bare mountain.

When the youngest of my three children was little, she'd arrange her bed sheets for snuggling in what she called her "nest." Whether a little girl or a teenager, she'd also come into the kitchen when I was fixing dinner, and we'd waltz together or try the swing. We held one another. Now she's a shiny new veterinarian who moved this summer from Texas to California to work in an all-female, all-feline clinic. The last years of vet school, she'd been too busy and happy to notice or consciously need the movable nest often. Parenting is a complex dance: sensing when to move in and suggest a few steps and when to step back and watch a daughter explore her unique dance. Well, I'd stepped back when I knew Cissy was moving confidently through her days, and we'd chatted weekly by phone as I do with her siblings. The graduation glow dimmed quickly, though, when she arrived nightly at her California apartment exhausted and overwhelmed to the company of her two large cats and her assertive Chihuahua. I imagined Cis folding her menagerie into her long arms and thinking, "What have I done? What have I done?" The familiar: classes, friends, boyfriend, professors with answers and encouraging words, her siblings and most of her family were miles away. Physically miles away.

I've begun taking yoga here in Santa Fe, and I watch an attentive instructor survey our group and discreetly offer a blanket or foam block for support. Through practice, she assesses what a particular torso needs to stretch more effectively and slips an aid below a struggling body. As I had stepped back in the improvised parental dance when I knew Cissy was moving confidently through her days, I needed again to be more present with phone calls, notes, emails reminding her of an old rhythm, the movable arc waiting to sustain and support her. She worked in her garden for solace, called to report on the blooms on her hibiscus, morning glory, geraniums.

The shelters we create often unconsciously, the incubators for difficult times or for a needed rest, like all animal nests, reveal ingenuity and adaptive behavior. I weave in what I've inherited, threads with Mexican patterns.

Though Mother wanted to be a writer and, due to the Depression, never had the opportunities she gave her children, she and my aunt, Lobo, instilled their love of language and books. Now Libby and I enjoy our first writing effort together, an exploration perhaps deeper than our conversations about books. I drink in the fresh taste of her bold voice. Words link us.

She begins a job search, and our dance rhythm changes.

Years ago I dreamed my beloved aunt, Lobo, the word that means wolf in Spanish. She was indeed our wolf-mother, who always returned home bearing Archie comics and Butterfingers. She would knock on our door, calling, "¿Dónde están mis lobitos? Where are my little wolves?" In the dream, she's fading away, and I know it, but I'm holding her up and holding on to her. I imagine my children one day propping me up, leading in the dance, their arms or delicious voices on the phone, my nest.

This sturdy yet imaginary construct, the movable nest, like prayer, requires faith and practice to become a habit. Without

4

attention, the fragile yet firm house unravels. The oldest of four, I scrutinize the web of relationships looking for spots that need patching. "You're a nester," my son says when I describe how my husband and I are decorating our New Mexico Casita de Flores, installing fountains in the small, shady garden; planting impatiens and ajuga in the shade. I keep a close eye on the butterfly bush planted in a sunny spot, the shrub that reminds me of Libby as do the Tibetan prayer flags she and her husband gave us. I imagine my family visiting, soaking up the sound of aspens rustling and bluejays calling, water splashing in the high desert breeze. I shape a space of rejuvenation, a haven for children and siblings, a retreat.

Sadly, my family is too far away from the glue of food much of the time, but summers and holidays provide the chance to gather the bodies I love together around the turkey and tamales for the non-vegetarians, the cranberry wine sauce and banana nut bread. Weekly, by phone, we knit us together. Our goodbyes are pauses in the shared life that I believe continues even after we shed these flesh envelopes, our bodies.

The wonder of life's mysteriès: we leave home, and we carry it with us; for some, a crushing weight; for others, a sturdy boat below the feet.

LIBBY MARTINEZ

Coming Home

There are no straight lines in my backyard. Each season, what used to be a square and orderly piece of lawn grows ever smaller, carved at the edges by undulating beds. The blades of thirsty St. Augustine now form a deep green "pool" in my shaded Austin garden.

The transformation of my yard started almost immediately upon my arrival to my first home away from home. I remember standing with my husband on our small concrete backyard stoop surveying the mass of neat green rectangles the builder had placed over the truckloads of sandy loam. Somehow the image didn't feel right. Although I had spent countless hours in the soupy Southern night air walking back and forth, back and forth over each soggy piece, praying for the roots to take hold, I decided that my little square yard was—well—it was just too square. It needed a little softening. Even though I am not the Pictionary partner anyone who wanted to win would choose, I set forth with pencil and tablet to draw what I saw in my mind. With the paper placed horizontally on what little furniture we owned at the time, I traced long, curving ribbons around the outside margins of the yard—the drawing looked like a cloud floating in a picture frame. When I finished what generously could be termed my landscape blueprint, I handed it to my husband. As his eyes moved over the lined paper, I remember saying to him, "Wait, I have a picture."

I left him sitting on our soft gray-green couch, the one which now sits in our study and serves as one of my cat's favorite napping places, as I went in search of one of the only items I would take if my house was burning down, my childhood photo album. Painstakingly created by my mother and given to me when I was twenty-one years old, it begins with my mom's actual hospital wristband which contains the time (7:26 P.M.) and date (May 13, 1970) of my birth in El Paso, Texas, and ends with a photo of my mom and me taken in what I think is the summer of 1990. We are both wearing white shirts, bright lipstick, and startlingly similar hairdos. I glance at the first pages of photos taken when I was an infant in a house I do not remember—me looking into a carved Halloween pumpkin (I have always loved the sweet, starchy smell), me blowing out the two candles on my pink-frosted birthday cake, me sitting next to my great aunt Lobo who always dressed in dark colors. And then I find it.

In the foreground I am flying down the backyard slide in the home we moved into when I was three. The photo was taken during my four-year-old *Wizard of Oz* birthday party. My brother had made the name tags for the many small guests. Although you can barely make out the outline of our brick grill (the one my sister delusionally remembers my father making Halloween cookies on) it would be hard to miss the soft curves of the flower beds—the same curves my husband was staring at on the thin notebook paper. There was my thick grass pool.

And so like a painter or sculptor who seeks to give form to her dreams, I have spent the better half of three years recreating the backyard of my childhood. Some of the plants nestled in the moist banks of cedar mulch were placed there purposefully—the pungent, purple-flowered vitex, the pink and white oleanders (I planted these even though the consumption of their poisonous leaves had proved to be the death of the guinea pigs I had when I was small), the sinewy desert willow which, true to its name, does not like my sticky clay soil, and the wisteria vine whose wild, chameleon green tendrils used to be the bane of my father's existence. Although I have planted many varieties of roses, I am always on the hunt for a type I cannot name but would know on sight. It is a bush with dozens of small, densely-packed pink blooms. Almost every time I go to a nursery with a roses section, I walk the damp gravel aisles in search of it. Some of my plants, like my glossy abelia, I was drawn to inexplicably at the time. But then, during one of her visits, my mom told me that one used to grow outside my bedroom window.

7

My mom now has a new garden in Santa Fe. During my recent visit, while savoring the cool night air, I walked along the crunchy path of her enclosed desert oasis—what she has recently named Casita de Flores. As I bent down to inspect the new additions to the pine-covered soil, I noticed the familiar elongated and veiny leaves of a diminutive butterfly bush. I have two in my Austin garden. It is one of my favorite plants because it blooms bright pink and purple, the colors I most want to be. A little green piece of me had migrated nine hundred miles back to the desert.

What other memories had seeped out of my skin and onto the canvas of my new home? Because I am an orderly person by nature, a maker of lists like both of my parents, I thought maybe a small inventory was in order. The gray-green couch which now serves as an expensive scratching post for my cat has been replaced by a rustic wooden scratch-proof version, just like the one which sat in my living room as a child, only with lighter-color wood. Although I am not blessed by floor-to-ceiling bookshelves, I have tried to recreate the densely packed and varied library which took up a whole wall in my den. According to the original blueprints, I think it was supposed to be a wet bar. Although I would frequently visit the local library with my mother, I remember thinking that, with all the books in my house, I would never run out of things to read. My current compulsion for buying books has outpaced the furniture requirement, and my husband and I are living amid many small, neatly stacked pyramids. These have been made topple-proof by thin layers of expertly placed *New Yorkers*. My bathroom is painted bright yellow, just like the one I shared, often begrudgingly, with my younger sister and older brother. I have also recreated the low, rhythmic humming of our swamp cooler which used to lull me to sleep as a child. I now have an air filter placed close to my bed. My mom says that I have always liked the sound of motors.

Lest the psychologists out there start worrying, there are many aspects of my house which are different than the home in which I spent my formative years. There are several more "junk" drawers, for instance, than I would like to publicly admit. A recent search through one revealed the following items: a compass, three almost identical pairs of scissors, a half-eaten box of Altoids, all gently cradled by a couple hundred pages of computer and appliance warranties, health insurance booklets, a printed version of the rules of chess, and the instructions for installing a drip watering system. I guess if anyone is ever lost, thinking of taking up papier-mâché after having eaten a loaf of garlic bread and wondering what their insurance co-payment is, whether a pawn can take a queen, or the size of their water meter, they have a source in Austin, Texas. Also, almost all of the rooms in my house are painted a different color. My kitchen, for instance, is a brilliant lapis blue that I just know will make a future real estate agent shudder.

It is in this sun-drenched blue kitchen that my attempts to more completely recreate my childhood home have fallen humorously short. Anyone who knows me and my lack of culinary acumen would find it hard to believe that I am genetically related to a woman who used to make decorative chocolate leaves for the top of her crème de menthe ("grasshopper") pie. I marvel at the impossibility of growing up alongside someone who made pecan tassies, trifle, divinity, and baked Alaska, when I'm still afraid to boil rice. For most of my married life, I have been relegated to the role of sous-chef—the chopper of tomatoes and the grater of cheese. If I did not have the good fortune of being married to an excellent chef I would probably have developed a mean case of scurvy. My husband's parting words before business trips used to be, "And remember, your dinner can't all be the same color." This was a cruel allusion to my past creative pairing of cornbread and macaroni. Although my mother used to come home from a full day's work and start dinner each night with her heels still on, it is a significant occasion in my house, usually preceded and followed by several days' vacation, when I make a complete meal. It is also an event I ensure that my husband Roger relays in detail to my mother-in-law thereby allaying my gnawing fears of domestic incompetence.

Although my mother feels completely at home in the kitchen

("It is my space," she recently told me), much to my disappointment, there is no joy for me in cooking, only fear. I am somewhat soothed by the fact that at least my younger sister shares this affliction. During one of our recent pre-Thanksgiving cooking extravaganzas using our family's favorite recipes, my husband, led by the piercing sound of the kitchen smoke detector, found us trying to rescue runny "sweet potato surprise" and an unruly batch of "cranberry wine sauce." My sister and I joke every year about making a *bûche de Noël* (complete with decorative meringue mushrooms), but it is probably a culinary experiment worthy of lowering my homeowner's insurance deductible. The ironic part is that, although I'm not very good at cooking, I spend quite a bit of time thinking about it. I love to read recipes in the latest magazines and cookbooks generously supplied by my mother while imagining myself effortlessly making béchamel sauce and bite-size crostini. Sometimes during the middle of the day, when I should be deciphering health care legislation, I gaze dreamily at computer images of marzipan fruit, pastry bags, and lattice crusts.

Just as some people resolve to become more patient and compassionate, I have resolved to become a better cook. And although that might sound trite and somewhat spiritually unambitious, for me it is not. It is like gardening; it is coming home. Sitting on the concrete stoop in my backyard, surrounded by sweet green memories, I send my hopes on the wings of brightly-colored Tibetan prayer flags into the twilight Texas sky. Down through the crisp New Mexico air they float and are caught on the colored cloth squares strung in my mother's arid garden. And I wait for the phone to ring, looking forward to listening to my mother explain the difference between blanching and boiling.

KATHERINE SMITH

LEÇONS DES TENEBRES

Four years of puberty have brought us to tonight's dinner:
onions fried in oil with tomato, coriander seed, cumin,

and chicken thighs. "Good, Mom," my daughter sings,
goes back to her boyfriend on the phone. I wash the dishes

we've used since we moved back to America,
listen to the wind hurl in winter dark outside the kitchen.

More than fifteen years ago in Paris
I slept in her father's arms, my belly ripe

as fruit and burned with desire
in a room gleaming with bleached pine

while a string quartet played Couperin on a June
morning. Now the knowledge that made her grows

distant as the bodies of fireflies that all summer
lit up the branches of the apple tree.

SHARON OLDS

HIGH SCHOOL SENIOR

For seventeen years, her breath in the house
at night, puff, puff, like summer
cumulus above her bed,
and her scalp smelling of apricots
—this being who had formed within me,
squatted like a bright tree-frog in the dark,
like an eohippus she had come out of history
slowly, through me, into the daylight,
I had the daily sight of her,
like food or air she was there, like a mother.
I say "college," but I feel as if I cannot tell
the difference between her leaving for college
and our parting forever—I try to see
this house without her, without her pure
depth of feeling, without her creek-brown
hair, her daedal hands with their tapered
fingers, her pupils dark as the mourning cloak's
wing, but I can't. Seventeen years
ago, in this room, she moved inside me,
I looked at the river, I could not imagine
my life with her. I gazed across the street,
and saw, in the icy winter sun,
a column of steam rush up away from the earth.
There are creatures whose children float away
at birth, and those who throat-feed their young
for weeks and never see them again. My daughter
is free and she is in me—no, my love
of her is in me, moving in my heart,
changing chambers, like something poured
from hand to hand, to be weighed and then reweighed.

LINDA PASTAN

LULLABYE FOR 17

You are so young
you heal as you weep,
and your tears
instead of scalding
your face like mine
absolve
simply as rain.

I tried to teach you
what I knew: how men
in their sudden beauty
are more dangerous,
how love refracting light
can burn the hand, how memory
is a scorpion

and stings with its tail.
You knew my catechism
but never believed. Now
you look upon pain
as a discovery all your own,
marveling at the way it invades
the bloodstream, ambushes sleep.

Still you forgive
so easily. I'd like
to take your young man
by his curls and tear
them out,
who like a dark planet circles
your bright universe
still furnished with curtains

you embroidered yourself,
an underbrush
of books and scarves,
a door at which
you'll soon be poised
to leave.

KATHRYN STRIPLING BYER

LAST DAY

S ummer's over, Sally says, as she leaves the pool with her young grandsons. My daughter still swims laps. It's two o'clock. The sun has only just begun to inch downward. The air is hot, unmoving. This could be any day of June, July, August, but it is this day, September 15, the last day the pool will be open.

When will they drain the water out? I ask. My daughter, the lifeguard, taking a break from her duties, shrugs as she treads water.

The image of an empty concrete pool surrounded by mountains as October comes on makes me sad. The notion of left-behind, empty spaces always does. I remember the last sigh of my grandmother's house before we drove away in the dusk, standing there like an abandoned part of ourselves. *Home is so sad,* Philip Larkin says. *It stays as it was left.* But he was wrong. When a year later the homeplace burned, we wailed out our grief. As we stood around the smoking ruins, my grandmother said over and over, "Thank God he didn't live to see this." My grandfather, who had held on to this homeplace through the Great Depression, supporting a family of six with farming and menial jobs in town, had died two years before. My uncle, who had worked the land since my grandfather's death, left the ruins there exposed, but then, he had never cared much for the place, ashamed of it. When my grandmother died, lots were drawn and my aunt got the homeplace.

Now the site is grassed over, the big oak trees surround a green clearing. A place for memory to expand in, not cringe before.

The space is empty, but air is supposed to be, isn't it?

Houses, pools, bedrooms, are not.

Why do they haunt me? Do we really leave behind part of ourselves in our places, some presence that waits, that pulls at us through the absence?

And why should I care about this pool where my daughter continues her laps—the plastic daisies whirring in a sudden breeze

15

as if this could be any day at all, not the last day?

I care because this is one of those landscapes from her child-hood and my motherhood. Here I sat under my favorite tree on a lounge chair reading or watching her stroke her way back and forth. Here I wept behind dark glasses during the summer before she left for college. Here I began poems, made grocery lists, listened to the distance out there among the clouds—something I hardly heard other places, rushing from stove to washing machine and supermarket.

On this last day, the 90-degree heat makes the mountains look hazy. The leaves are beginning to turn slightly russet. The university students at their classes down the road are already a month into their term.

My daughter has two more weeks to go till we load her up for another drive to Chicago. Another year of looking toward Thanks-giving, Christmas, Spring break. Summer again.

When I went away to school, I lived only three hours away. Weekend visits were monthly events. One early Monday morning as I began to pull away from the house, my father came toward the car, bending over as if he wanted to tell me something. I rolled down the window but not quickly enough for his hasty kiss. We kissed through the glass, and embarrassed, I drove off, with his words still in my ears: *Now it's all meeting and parting.* Did he know he was lifting from Frost?

The love of parent for child is the heaviest I've known. The cinder block of it pulls me under the surface of these late summer days over and over again. I rise with my eyes wet, the weight of the salt sea in my chest.

That terrible burden of love, as Eavan Boland described it years ago, phoning me from Ireland to confirm a reading engagement. We had daughters the same age, and I had wondered how she could bear having a whole ocean between them. My own mother rarely went anywhere without us when we were young, and when she did, a one-night trip to Atlanta, she was so overcome with emotion that she buried her head in her hands as the car drove away.

16

The smell of coconut oil sunscreen calls back the pools of childhood. The creek where we went to swim, the poor pretense of it, neither a pool nor beach, a country person's version, the sand squishing through our toes, the water full of minnows, an occasional fish. My mother and aunts on towels on the banks, remembering their own summer days by this water.

The wind blows the water into a pattern, a choppy glyph of waves. They mingle with the wake stirred by my daughter's passing. Her feet churn up diamonds, a brilliance that subsides into, ultimately, nothing. The drops on her black Chicago cap glisten as she passes; at the end she kicks off again, laps, flip turns and swims back toward me.

The place is deserted now, save for the two of us. This is the way she likes it. No children screaming, no mothers letting them run wild, no boys lunging in. This is our place. She swims. I watch.

What are you writing? A poem? She is watching me, hanging on to the edge of the pool.

Just writing, I say.

Another turning. So many. And it does no good to tell me I must learn to let go. Letting go is what we spend our lives doing, whether we want to or not, whether or not we learn how to do it.

Tomorrow the pool will be closed for another year.

In two weeks we will drive away from our house, the dogs, the trees, the late afternoon that in other days would announce suppertime, a glass of wine, chips on the table, news on NPR.

And in two days after that, we will turn away from her standing in her small dorm room crammed with her things and drive back into another late afternoon, the traffic beginning to worsen, over the Skyway bridge into Indiana and as far into the night as we can before my husband gets too tired to drive. We will turn on the television in our motel room, sip bourbon from plastic motel cups, and I, for one, be relieved that one more parting is over with, the solitary life open again, the books, the poems, time to be wife, teacher, writer, all the things taken over by Mother.

And she will be whoever she is. Daughter only a small part of

17

it. We will float on the surface most days, the awful burden of love lessened a while, the cinder block barely noticed, the imagination opening up to other things, first things or coming back things.

I will clean house for hours. Allowed entry, I will air her room, go through her belongings, launder her linens. I will throw out old clothes. Cast off more of her childish things.

I will take walks with my husband, plan my days around us, not her, believing that as she journeys toward her freedom, her own life, so do I.

Another summer gone. The mid-afternoon wind rises. The hawks ride it above the mountains.

Memory, I am learning, is not dependable. Daily things slip from its grasp. I know that most of this day will flicker out. But not too soon. I remember a poem by Margaret Atwood, the sister watching her younger sister ice skate, the brilliance of the moment. The final line.

Over all I place a glass bell.

CORINNA L. BYER

CITRONS

Behind a wooden fence,
      Age-old, which twines
           Around my grandfather's farm
Like a smiling serpent
      Lies a field I saw only once—
           My eyes still adjusting to the light.
"Citrons," my mother explained
      To me about the yellow melons
           Lying among the cornhusks
As if they were failed soldiers
      Dying on a battlefield
           With only a bed of leaves.

Later I took one back with me
      Throwing it up as one throws confetti,
           As my cousin and I tossed
Weeds and flowers at each other long ago.
      Yes, I decided, I'd take it away with me—
           Far away, like my mother who left
This very same farm, years before my birth,
      Suitcase still in her hands.

ANDRÉE CHEDID

BRÈVE INVITÉE
à ma fille

Ma lande mon enfant ma bruyère
Ma réelle mon flocon mon genêt,
Je te regarde demain t'emporte
Où je ne saurais aller.

Ma bleue mon avril ma filante
Ma vie s'éloigne à reculons,
A toi les oiseaux et la lampe
A toi les torches et le vent.

Mon cygne mon amande ma vermeille
A toi l'impossible que j'aimais
A toi la vie, sel et soleil,
A toi, brève invitée.

ANDRÉE CHEDID

So Briefly, My Guest
to my daughter

My moor my child my heather
My real one my snowflake my wild flower,
I watch tomorrow carry you off
Where I can never follow.

My azure my April my free one
My life recedes into the past,
For you, are the birds and the lamp
For you, are the torches and wind.

My swan my almond my amber
For you, are the dreams I once loved
For you, life, its salt and its sun,
For you, so briefly, my guest.

*Translated from the French by Judy Cochron,
in collaboration with Renée Linkhorn*

JEANNETTE CABANIS-BREWIN

CHRISTMAS DAY: MAX PATCH BALD

On the summit, a smooth, grassy island anchored
in swells of white cloud. Like castaways, we lie
on the welcoming ground, dark coats gathering
thin sunshine. She lay her head on my heart.
The azure dome spun around that stillpoint.
When she sprang up, sudden runaway,
her dog manfully followed on short, faithful legs.

I could only stand and wait, watching for her,
glimpsing her across the rising and falling
billows of that exalted earth. Her silhouette
emerged, a slip of shadow, before the blinding
glitter of rimed north-facing slopes. Then
she disappeared, gone over the rim of the world.
I blew on my fingers, stamped the earth like a patient mare.

Soon she bobbled back into view, skipping, carrying
a withered bouquet of yellow nightshade fruits,
the dog merry at her side.

This is what it means now, to be her mother:
moments intimate as once she lay beneath my heart.
Long times of distancing and disappearance.
Then, clearing the horizon, a joyful sailing-closer—
a wave, a smile—a turn in the path and she sinks out of view.
She is out there, and in good company, safe for now though bearing
the world's deadliest poison like a golden scepter before her.

ALICE FRIMAN

LETTING GO

My mother's favorite word was "No." Up to her death at ninety-five and through all those years of my growing up. "No" and its many incarnations. "Not now." "Not yet." "You can't." "You shouldn't." Or her more subtle versions of frowning disapproval: "You're never satisfied," "You don't really mean that," or the worst, "If you do that, you'll only be disappointed." I was doomed before I started. My father, who had a streak of joy in him, often grumbled that she was a "wet blanket." I remember coming across a joyous note I had sent her back in 1986 when an early poem of mine had been selected for *Keener Sounds: Selected Poems from The Georgia Review*. She had written on the bottom, "When the gods want to punish you, they answer your prayers."

I am being too hard on her. Perhaps all those negatives were the only way she knew to handle her fear, her way of saying, "I'm afraid for you, your *I want I want*, your outrageous energy." This is not to say she was a bad mother, anything but. I adored her. But she was fearful and a homebody at heart. When I asked her once why oh why she'd married my father, a difficult man at best, her answer was that she had wanted a little apartment of her own to fix up just as her beloved older sister had done. If her ambitions reached further than that in 1927 when she was twenty-two, she didn't seem to know it. The Roaring Twenties with its *bo-dee-o-do* and slipping-the-traces seemed to have passed her by. And when my sister was born in 1929, she buckled herself into those traces with a vengeance, probably going at motherhood too hard.

Coming four years later, I was luckier, an "easier" baby, as they used to say, but luckier, yes, because I was left more to my own devices. Later, when she used to go to work at Clover Towel, the family business, and wasn't home every day when I got home from school, I was *especially* lucky. What did I do in those days before TV, those blessed afternoons? Devour a bag of McIntosh apples while reading in the big green chair, paint, or turn on the radio and dance for hours. Life was the big adventure I found in books and in the possibility found on every New York City street where I hoped to be "discovered," especially as I walked once a week to The Jules Stone Dance Studios on 181st Street, daydreaming and never looking where I was going. No wonder she worried.

But what's this got to do with this anthology and this essay I admit to writing under duress, sure it will not fit into a collection devoted to the empty-nest syndrome, because, if the truth be known, I never had an empty-nest syndrome. Writing that last sentence makes me feel a bit like Hester Prynne outside the jail-house door with her telltale *A*. But I am getting ahead of myself.

I gave birth to three children, and never wished for anything beyond that each baby be healthy. After nine months—nine and a half with the first—boy, girl, what's the difference? I am not senti-mental. My father used to sit in the theater when I danced and weep. He'd stand in the back of the school auditorium when I'd recite in oratory contests and wipe his eyes with a big white hand-kerchief. "See," Mother would say, "how he really does love you." I was very young when I learned the difference between easy tears and the ones I sobbed into the bathroom towels for hours, for years.

All I knew was, I was happy only when I created happy. That what I saw and experienced was never what others saw and expe-rienced, and certainly not what Mother told me I was seeing and feeling. All my life I've been trying to explain myself. Perhaps this essay is just more of the same, another way to do just that.

But as I was saying, I had three children—two boys and a girl, in that order. By the time the first, Richard, was born, I had left New York City, my home since the beginning of forever, and set-tled, much to my shock and challenge, in the midwest. Paul came three years later, my daughter, Lillian, four years after that. Was I pleased the baby was a girl? Thinking I only made boys, I was more like amazed. Unlike Paul who howled as soon as his mouth hit the air and her brother Richard who was probably too drugged by what they had given me to voice much of anything, she yelped once as if to comply, then, I swear, took a long look around. I should have known then she'd turn out to be a photographer.

But did I love her more or differently than I did the boys? I can't say that. Was her personality inherently different because she was female? I can't even say that. She seemed tougher than they were, feistier, more social, but that could only be that as a third child, she had to be. But I know this—I was determined to treat her no differently than I did her brothers. And no, I never hankered after little ruffled dresses and white lace socks, although I must admit I was a bit disconcerted when the black birth hair that grew perpendicular to her head was replaced, not with the golden curls of one of her brothers or the silver platinum of the other, but with a nondescript brown that also grew, porcupine fashion, perpendicular to her head.

During the early years of her life, the women's movement was finally seeping into Indiana—articles in magazines, talk on the radio, consciousness-raising groups. It was a heady time. And this new girl child of mine was, because I was, bound to be caught up in it. The year after Lillian was born, I started back to school. Because my husband didn't like the idea (I imagine he felt threatened), he asked sarcastically who was going to pay for it. "Not you," I said, and went to work on the weekends, teaching at the temple and running their assembly programs. In addition, I started a little drama group, the plays I wrote, all religious satires. Wicked, wicked. That and the monthly article I wrote for a local newsletter, the three kids, the garden, the meat loaf, the big house to clean, and, oh yes, all those starched white cotton shirts to be ironed. Later, women like me were called the Amazons. Maybe for all I know, that whole generation of women had mothers like mine whose favorite word was NO. Maybe all we really wanted was that our lives should in the end add up to something—a big YES. You want this mountain moved across the street? It's blocking the sun from your petunia? Sure. No problem.

During the first years of Lillian's life, I was back in school, one

25

night a week, pursuing a degree in literature. Since the boys were in school, this meant structuring my day around her meals, her outings, and especially her afternoon nap when I could get in three solid hours of study time. All vacuuming, bed-making, cooking, and scrubbing had to be finished by noon. Each morning I'd race through the house, cleaning, and she, of course, "helping," tagging along. One day as I was on my knees scouring out the upstairs bathtub, she, seeking to please and never observing me do anything else with such energy as clean, said, "Do you know what I want to be when I grow up?" No, what? "I want to be a maid." I stared at her little four-year-old face in horror. "You will be a nuclear physicist and *like* it," I yelled. Poor daughter. Poor girl child. Whatever was I about? All she was saying was she wanted to be just like her mother. And I, instead of my mother's adamant NO, had substituted another kind of no, a no that meant YES. No wonder she was confused. Once, a friend asked me, "What makes you think your children should be any different than anyone else's?" I didn't answer, but I know what that answer was. *Because they were mine.* Talk about willfulness.

Looking back, I think I was a cheerleader mother. Yes, you can. Of course you can. Get up, try again. There were boundaries, sure—chores; a curfew to meet (or there better be a phone call); extra money to be earned, not just given. But within those boundaries, the operative word was YES. School was the priority. I remember when my son was in seventh grade and wanting to give up Latin. (My reaction would have been the same had it been French or Spanish.) His argument was, he didn't need Latin because he was going to be a helicopter pilot. "Fine," I said. "But you'll be the first helicopter pilot who can speak Latin."

But if being imperious usually worked on the boys, it wouldn't be enough for Lillian. The problem was, in a time when I was told I couldn't get into graduate school because of my "age and sex" (I was 38), how could I make her courageous enough, resilient enough, and battle-ready enough to leave when it was time for her to go? And I guess I felt, and still do, that *that* is a parent's hardest job: to open the front door. To be the one that opens that door, not waiting until the child feels he or she has to bang it down in order to leave. If I was a "good mother," my *reward* would be an empty house, not my sorrow. I trained them to be independent. Yes I did. I just made sure that the tether let out a little at a time, never more than they could handle, but never got so long and loose that they'd be lost and not able to feel the steel post, me, at the other end.

It would be comforting if we could agree on a definition of what constitutes a good mother. The Victorian model, for instance, of self-sacrifice—the bird who pecks her own breast until it bleeds. You know, "I've worked my fingers to the bone"—that variety. I remember seeing a segment on *60 Minutes* showing how that paragon of virtue is alive and well. In Italy, sons of forty, fifty years old choosing to remain home with Mama who still makes their bed, picks up their dirty underwear, cooks for them, cleans. One son who lives in another city even ships his laundry home each week for her to wash, iron, and ship back in a box. And these are men with money and careers, some with their own houses.

But the revelation came when Leslie Stahl interviewed the mothers. Taking care of their sons *was* their life. The idea of a life motivated by one's own center, by one's own talents and desires and push toward self-realization seemed never to have occurred to them. I wonder how in her youth, each dealt with the loss of herself as she was in the process of giving it up. I'm reminded of my cousin whose life *is* her children. When you call her on the phone and ask, after her litany of what's doing with the kids, yes, but how are *you*, there's no *you* there. Paul Gauguin, the postimpressionist, posed this question: how much sense does it make that a parent give up his life for the children so that those children can grow up to give up their lives for *their* children who, in turn, give up *their* lives, and on and on. I think of my grandmothers and great-grandmothers, that long string going back, back, each giving up who knows what desire or hope or ambition for the questionable joy of knowing that their children and their children's children will grow up to do the same.

I wanted each of my children to have a life, difficult maybe, but a real one nonetheless. That was my wish for them. The actualization of that wish was not as simple or as easy as one would hope.

Imagine, my daughter, the youngest, until the age of twelve sitting at a dining room table each evening surrounded by her family—five of us. And probably like every other family in America, singing in the car:

> Oh! we ain't got a barrel of money,
> Maybe we're ragged and funny,
> But we'll travel along
> Singing a song
> Side by side...

Within two years, it would all disappear. What to her must have seemed carved in granite, vanished. The separation, the messy divorce, first one brother off to college then the other, and then the sudden death of her father, forty-eight years old. Abracadabra. Now you see it, now you don't. Five people reduced to two. The whole family, down the rabbit hole. What could she know of that long, slow dying of a marriage? And what difference would it have made to her back then?

There were just the two of us now, and we were in it for the long haul. And it was a long haul. There was one year I didn't think she'd live—two car accidents, her bad choice of men, her illness, her hospitalizations, the certainty that she lived under an unlucky cloud that would not move. And there were experiences I'd sooner forget. When she was fifteen, a man too old for her got too close, taking advantage, and I threatened him. And later, when she was so sick and hounded by the man who gave her nightmares for years, I did it again. My maternal feelings for this child weren't anything like sacrificial. They were ferocious. The idea of pining in a daughter's empty room of lace and high-school posters makes me hoot. I'd have killed for that child. Make no mistake about it.

The empty-nest syndrome is the sense of sorrow and loss experienced when the child leaves home, especially when that leaving entails suitcases and lots of boxes. Perhaps the leaving, even if it is only for that first college semester, represents for the mother a separation reminiscent of, if not a symbolic reenactment of, that first separation, and that's why it can cause such pain: empty nest syndrome/postpartum blues.

Because I went to a New York City college, there being no other choice, I didn't leave home until I got married. Did my mother experience an empty nest? I don't know. I only know on the day I graduated, she was angry with me, and I never knew why. And a year later, before I got married, she had periodic bouts of anger. "Who will I talk to?" she'd say. And for months after the wedding, I was accused of being "selfish," "not paying attention," forgetting about her. If Anne Sexton was right ("A woman *is* her mother./ That's the main thing.") then the mother voice in my head is the one I strive *against*. But perhaps she was right. I am selfish. I wanted for my children what I always wanted for myself—to experience their short time in the world as an adventure. When my son Paul was born, I watched in the mirror how as soon as his mouth hit the air, he let out a great cry, and I raised up on my elbows, leaned back my head, and laughed for the sheer joy of it.

Think of the imagery. When giving birth, you essentially, with a massive heave and strain, push the baby out. And if you follow that metaphor as it repeats itself over and over down the long corridors of motherhood, it eventually and inevitably leads to the door marked GO. To have my daughter who had been through so much walk out that door with confidence and the wholeness it would take to grab on to experience and weave it into the fabric of a life—*her* life—was joy indeed. Believe me, there was nothing empty in this house.

Lillian Elaine Wilson.
Alice Friman and daughter, Lillian Elaine Wilson, 2007.
Photograph.

LILLIAN ELAINE WILSON

LEAVING MOTHER

I.

On the stoop, I peer
through the locked screen door
making binoculars of my hands.
It's hazy-muted, this sun-faded colander
tiny gray squares sift out your silhouette.

A familiar anxiety from childhood rises,
calls out to rattle the handle,
Or kick, with banging knocks
against the solid dented metal base.
I am bouncing flies, from the shaking
disturbing their grid-pacing
on this ladder, this gate.

Inside, you write poetry.
Like the spider here, decorating the porch light
building your own intricate bug net
clinging to silky messages
dangling a moment, from my disturbance
stomping legs approach, across a webbed floor
a warning upon entry
before starting in once more.

In the same room
now, or 20 years later
matter that doesn't much
I am a lamp, a pillow, a piano leg
finished, created like one of your poems
taking on my own life, worked through,
and time to be sent out.

If I come back
you'll send me out again.

II.

Ready,
pushing away, capable now
ending the always hoping for the creak of an old hinge.
I want you to know before YOU go
that everything I will need
waits safely in the lines of your poetry
a great gift
your love, erasing the rusty grid dust
off my dreamy nose with your thumb.

III.

I'll leave our voices nested
in a windowed door, compartmented forever
the inside or out question of it,
coming and going
at the last touch of the house,
I'll close it slowly with a compressed click.

SARAH GORHAM

A WOMAN DRAWN TWICE

L aura, eldest daughter of two, driver of a Toyota as old as she is, occupant of the attic room, is going off to college. My friends are all sympathetic. I must be a bad parent because this imminent separation doesn't strike me as tragic.

What's made it easier is Laura herself. She holds the world at arm's length. Even as a baby, Gram, Dad, and I were the only ones she'd allow to touch her. Uncles and aunts, forget it. Her very first sentence, as her father tried to pry the flap loose from her diaper, was "Don't do that!"

Once she was allowed to bring her friend Rita along to our summer place in Wisconsin. For three days they were inseparable, sunbathing together on the pier, riding their bikes to town for vanilla malts. And then suddenly Laura had had enough social bonding. She began to sleep in, to disappear on mysterious after-dinner walks. One morning I took my cup of tea to the edge of the lake, and there was poor Rita, splashing about in a rowboat, forlorn and abandoned.

Laura keeps a journal, leaves it on the coffee table or on the bathroom floor. Perhaps to lure us inside, perhaps not. But we don't look. She also has a webpage and there with a click of a button we are welcomed in, browsers like anyone else. It doesn't feel like trespassing, but the voice we hear is not meant for us:

"Hello beautiful this is Laura the 16 year old illegal permit driving, Manual High School attending, singing, dancing, romancing Ramsi's employee. I read, write, and wish every day that precalculus didn't exist. I'm out every weekend, sorry to you silly fools that get online 24/7 no I don't want to be your friend. Why do people love those bland, uninteresting talentless 'artists' they see on television? That was cynical...and yuck, no I'm not a lesbian. I'm going to be an English professor of creative writing at NYU with three novels, a wealthy, but interesting husband im in love with and a kid or two in my spare time. You have a problem with it you can call my super expensive top of the line lawyer, wherever he is."

I can hardly believe what I'm reading. Evidence of a double life! This is completely foreign to me, for I was a loud-mouth child, an acter-out, a show-off. At sixteen I told my mother everything and opened my heart to anyone else who would listen too. Because in my mind, a kept secret was a festering thought, dangerous to my health.

•

My mother was a gentle soldier at the kitchen sink, a doe with ears twitching. Faithful and loving, available for all crises, transitions, triumphs. Still, I remember little about my own college lift-off. Only this: Luggage in hand, we approached the dorm—Cory Hall—and it was ugly. Tattered vinyl sofas in the lobby, graffiti on the cinderblock walls, gray-green drapes half up, half down. There was something evil-smelling dripping from a balcony, and we had to dodge it to get in. *Oh Sarah* my mother said, her voice drooping at the end. But this Midwestern hippie school was my choice and it had to be a good one, so I was cheerful. *It's okay!*—my eyes distracted by two boys with long hair. And then she was gone.

And now I see her orange VW bus pull into the driveway and she enters the house again which is much the same as before. There is the smoked turkey on the counter which my mother remembers Sarah loves between two slices of Wonder Bread. There are the jeans with their U.S. flag patches which caused such an argument. There are the hairclips, the Prell shampoo, the mildewed camping equipment. Wandering from room to room, she gathers up the debris. She soaks up the silence and wonders why the storm that was her daughter's adolescence felt so unnavigable.

But I am just imagining things. Perhaps she simply turns to the next child, Nancy, with less than two years to go.

•

Laura has lost her sculpture. At first glance it looked like a stone thumb, but on closer inspection was actually quite moving—a tiny figure stooped in prayer or under the weight of a great burden. She kept it in a shoebox on the stairs, but now only the sandpaper and tools are there. She's frantic and of course it's all my fault for cleaning up. Tomorrow the sculpture is due in 3D art! Turns out the dog had carried it outside and is gnawing on it noisily. We approach him and he rumbles low in his throat.

Laura in the backseat, complaining about Cézanne. I think his paintings are ugly. He's way overrated. His portrait of the Alps looks like a big lump of ham, she says. My husband suggests she look at his other work before she condemns him completely. Yeah, yeah, she drones. *I'm sick of the Impressionists. Public schools love them. Humanities and Impressionism. French and Impressionism. Art and Impressionism. Blah Impressionism Blah.*

"Poor little melon, tossed in with the black turnips" (Chinese Proverb).

•

Years ago, passing by her room while Laura "napped," we'd hear a complex drama in several voices, high and low. "Jesus, I'm making a lot of noise," she once said to herself. Later, when she began to read, the theater went deeper inside. She breezed through all of Roald Dahl, folded up like a frog under her kindergarten desk. Her teacher reported this one day with a wry smile, then added generously, "Okay with me, as long as she's reading." By adolescence it was *The Idiot, Laughter in the Dark,* and *Light in August.* At fifteen, she showed us her first short story, "Climbing Out," written for an English class, about a girl who leaves a bad relationship with her boyfriend. We were taken aback by its sophistication—the wry, clear voice from one so young:

Eric stood up and climbed into the back of his '97 Ford pickup truck, his jeans clinging to the Tommy Hilfiger emblem on his boxer shorts. I had been dating Eric for over eight months and not once during that time had he ever used a belt. In addition, his idea of good conversation was a discussion on the gayness of our history teacher, Mr. Higgens.

"Hey Josie, what about his new toupee, is the horse hair real or faux this time?" he called from the truck.

His pointed smile sometimes reminded me of the Trix rabbit.

"I don't know," I replied.

She'd never even *had* a boyfriend, as far as I knew. Suddenly I felt exposed. Proud, but also afraid.

•

My mother too had a literary life. I know because of the pencil marks in her Modern Library edition of Frost, her poems around his poems. I know because I discovered her thesis, red-leather bound, carbon-copied on onion skin, Peggy Aring's analysis of Melville's *Billy Budd*. I know because one day a tall, gangly, middle-aged poet named Donald Peterson showed up at our front door. In his book from Wesleyan, which he was carrying, he called her his muse. And did you know she wrote too, he said to me. My mother flushed and wished him away. She wouldn't want me to tell you. But remember, I can't keep a secret.

My husband, a collector, purchases a "safety pen" circa 1904, its case sterling, about three-quarters of an inch in diameter. It looks like a fancy cigar tube, but twist a knob at the base and the 14-karat gold nib emerges from the chamber.

•

An hour of solitude in my house occupied by teenagers. It's three in the afternoon. I'm home from work and relishing *Carmen*, an arrangement for flute and piano on my radio. It speeds up my thinking, makes me want to dance. Laura is just now waking up. She appears puffy-eyed at my study door in her cabbage patch pajamas. *Mom. Mom. MOM. Would you turn that music off? It sounds like "Pop Goes the Weasel." Why would you want to hear that first thing in the A.M.?*

•

It's Mother's Day and by evening Laura has finally pulled some-thing together. She swipes one of my greeting cards and attaches a carnation, snipped from a bouquet I purchased that morning to cheer myself up. Later, feeling a little sheepish, she leaves a pot of petunias on the front hallway floor. *Is this for me?* I have to ask.

I scour the literature. "The child absorbs such a lot of lies and foolish nonsense, mixed in with essential truths, that the first duty of the adolescent who wants to be healthy is to disgorge it all." What they neglect to say is how well adolescence readies the *parent* for separation. Here are the words to that song: *Why don't you make Bonnie walk the dog? Why are you always harping on me? Do you have to eat right next to me? Why do you have to chew so loud?*

In Chinese characters, "woman" drawn twice signifies "quarrel."

•

Laura is working at Baskin Robbins four days a week, despite her intention to "be as irresponsible as I can this summer." Spare time is spent sleeping, on the computer IM-ing her friends, shopping at thrift stores. Obligation to family or chores gets short shrift. So too eating. The bowl of muddy milk left on the living room floor—Cocoa Krispies and skim—is the only evidence she's had any nourishment at all.

The pendulum begins to swing. Back. My mother was ashamed of her body. Forth. I kept a list of my lovers in a little black notebook. Back. Laura locks the bathroom door to wash her hands. Again: my mother picked at her food, pretending to be content with the turkey back, the wing. I claimed the breast, ate ravenously. Now, I stand guard over Laura to make sure she finishes her dinner. And on and on.

Why are you such a Hitler, she asks.

•

Laura wants to drive to Morehead to camp with her friends. Eastern Kentucky woods in an unreliable eighteen-year-old Toyota. The morning news influences our decision. A stripper in New Jersey pulled off the road when her car broke down. As she checked under the hood, she was blindsided by a passing vehicle. The driver kept going. So did the next three, even after they felt the jolt of her body under their wheels.

And the young man accepted at Yale who fell asleep and careened over a cliff in Colorado. And the teenagers and the country roads without yellow lines. And the dark. And Laura on the spearmint green lake at Disney World in her own little powerboat careening about like a demented waterbug. The wake of the ferry. Rocks. The other boats. And Laura traversing the waterfall, Laura with her nonchalant springy step, her inexplicable mixture of shyness and daring. Her parents holding their breath.

So, no. No, no, no. While your father and I can still say it. *No*.

Though my mother said *no* too and I trotted downstairs to my bedroom with its strung up Christmas ornament like a modern-day gazing ball. Then cranked the little wheel on my window and slipped out. Rob and his stepvan, his pot, his sexual hands, and the frenzy of cicadas were there to meet me in the dense Washington night.

Laura comes home with a red mark like a cherry lozenge at the base of her neck. She was supposed to be sleeping at Danielle's house. Just who gave her the hickey? Danielle? Not that I have a leg to stand on, which is why my outrage is tinged with hilarity. The Chinese are right: kids are creditors collecting for the sins of our past lives.

•

Again, I have the dream, not uncommon among women. Back at college for the summer term. The Ohio heat is suffocating, grass brown and rigid as toothpicks. Students less than half my age move about without even a glance in my direction. And why not, I'm not interesting; I'm too old to be there. But I've forgotten to turn in my paper for some literature class, or take that last PE credit (here the details vary), so my degree is at risk. Where's my family, everything I've accomplished? I'm nothing and the countryside too has lost its landmarks, a uniform beige surrounding the college like Beirut.

●

Several short stories later, my husband and I agree that Laura needs more than her public-school-24-year-old-baseball-coach-disaster-of-an-English-teacher can provide. We sign her up for the Reynolds Young Writers Workshop at Denison University, where she will study with Erin McGraw, a real fiction writer. She receives a large scholarship and before we know it, we're in the airport gently pressing a reluctant sixteen-year-old towards the boarding gate. She won't let us kiss her good-bye, annoyed that we've forced her into this. But a quick glance before she disappears into the plane reveals all—she's terrified. I let my husband drive home, too upset, convinced we should never have forced her into this. "Never have ideas about children," said D.H. Lawrence. "Never have ideas *for* them." See? See?

Three days pass and an e-mail finally arrives from Denison. Subject heading: "Blue Haired Freaks Can Suck My Bumper." (No explanation.)

"Family! How are things? Last evening Erin McGraw gave a reading from her unpublished new novel. We are the first *ever* to hear the opening chapter. She is an amazing writer and even with the typically short attention span that dominated this particular audience, every one of us listened with awe…My story is going to be workshopped on Sunday. I'm really struggling with the implausibility of this one. I wanted to concentrate on the plot as opposed to character but I made the mistake of writing it in the first person instead of third…OH, and at 2:00 A.M. we TPed the TA lounge and called random room numbers unpleasantly waking anyone that had gone to bed…"

She was ecstatic, knee deep in the jubilate of an unmanufactured epiphany. On the phone she gushed: "I've learned more in one day than I did in *four years* at Manual. Dad, do you know Flannery O'Conner? She is *awesome...*" Her intellect was on fire, just the sort of experience she needed to anchor the indefinite future. Now she had a signpost outside the home.

•

On July 30, 1980, during one of the hottest summers in D.C. history, my mother died of cervical cancer. For over a month, my sisters and I had shared the task of keeping her comfortable. We said our goodbyes in our caretaking—freshening her glass of chipped ice, reading E.B. White's letters to her, transcribing her farewell notes. She declined all medical treatment, hastened the end by refusing to drink. Her intention, I think, was to ease our burden, but it meant there was little time for the many questions we had. And no time of course for our future husbands, grandchildren, careers, the accomplishments she could be proud of. After she was gone, I kissed her cooling cheek. It seemed as conclusive a farewell as there could be.

Little did I know that in dreams and daylight visions, she would return again, a diminished version of herself. She dressed in a blue-and-white-striped garden apron, jeans, and clogs. A mother with a prolonged cold, a chronic disease, but content in her new life. She lived in Portugal, in Southern France, or, lately, in Greenland. Once, I could feel her hanging on the roof of our Toyota as we sped up the coast to Connecticut.

And now she appears in Laura's long legs, her splayed feet, and angled posture. My mother's chiseled Lutheran nose catches me by surprise when Laura cuts her bangs, or ties back her hair. She hates to hear this stuff, doesn't want to be associated with a dead person she never knew.

Besides, there's a difference. Next summer Laura will circle back, but not as a ghost. As an empowered, not a diminished being. This reassures, also unsettles me, for isn't this the natural order? And, isn't it my place she's taking?

In the new and improved dorm room at Laura's college, complete with microwave oven, tiny refrigerator, and private bathroom (tuition etc. has increased by a whopping 700% since I went to school), I'll be steeled for the big moment. I don't expect much—a ritual peck on the cheek which she will then quickly wipe off.

I'll drive the van home, park under the hackberry tree, if I'm lucky and there's a spot. The house will stay much the same. There are crumbs from her onion bagel and video games spread out on the floor. She never did learn to put them away. There's the Oxyclean, Q-tips, spray of face powder across the sink. The ubiquitous collapsed pajamas. I'm not imagining things—she's gone, and the time for grieving is underway. Or, perhaps I'll turn to her sister Bonnie, ready to inherit Laura's room, her car, her status at the grown-up one. Bonnie, with less than two years to go.

INGRID WENDT

ON THE NATURE OF TOUCH

My daughter's cat in the morning, before he'll eat,
needs to be picked up and petted, cradled (as I used to
carry my daughter) on one hip from pantry to counter
and back to the dish of food that was fresh the first
time he sniffed it, but not good enough.

This cat can be roaming all night, returning ravenous.
This cat can be let outside at first light and stand, moon-
patient, at the door, in rain, until we rise again. His fur
can be six soggy layers of needles and moss on the floor of the
        Oregon
coast range and still the Salmon Supreme we spoon into his dish
holds that scrupulous tongue only an instant before his voice
stalks our slippers, our wonder again at such
hunger for touch that goes beyond all bodily need.

So we stroke him between the ears, stirring up the same food.
And we rub his nose just over the spot where the whiskers
        sprout,
run our hands repeatedly down the long rapids of his spine
until dander and fur rise like spume, drift in the imperceptible
breath of the furnace, saying Good cat, Good Pillow, Eat.

And my daughter, who hardly could wait to be out on her own,
phones from her student apartment once, maybe twice a day, to
        ask for my
stroganoff recipe, or if vinegar will, in the absence of cleanser,
clean a greasy sink. She reads me the funnies.
Will I give her a ride to the store? Each day, this

delicate sniffing the ground called *home*; the words we speak
a ritual independent of meaning: thin fingers sifting the rich

humus of memory: bright
splashes of hair dye she left behind
on the downstairs hall carpet, each color a different
year of her life: stones scattered by Gretel to find the way back.
There is no returning to where she has been. How can I
not cradle her; each time she calls, one more blessed

delay on the long, slow road from touching each of us took
for granted those years I held her in my arms at least once a day
and she held me in a gaze that knew nothing but trust: water
disappearing through cracks in my fingers I myself tried, as a
    child,
over and over to cup and drink clear in my small, close hands.

HILDA RAZ

SARAH AMONG ANIMALS

—Priam's Green Birdwing

Night. The elephant in his pen
waits patiently for Sarah.
His vast ears inflate like sails
as his head, the size of a ship,
veers toward her compound.
His great foot lifts.

Among her butterflies,
a golden handkerchief bordered
with jet draped on her fist,
Sarah listens. She wants to go.
In her veins the thin blood flows.
Were she able to enter the field of light
her arms would flood with veins, and lift.
She lifts her shoulders, shrugs off his charge.
Night. The arc sails on.

LAUREN K. ALLEYNE

How to Leave Home

I.

July 13, 1997

It is the Sunday before I leave Trinidad for New York. I am only
supposed to be going for four years, but it is understood that it
may be much longer. A solemn day. My mother is busy preparing
the house and the prayer-room, while my father works in the
kitchen putting the final garnishes on the food that he has been
cooking for hours. My brother is in a white shirt and shorts, bike
ready, in case he has to do any last minute fetching or carrying, his
white pants pressed and neatly hanging over his bedroom door.
My sister sullenly arranges flowers for the altar—her least favorite
job because she hates the ants and insects that crawl out from the
freshly picked ginger lilies and bougainvillea, but she has a flair
for it and cannot stand the mess I make of the job. I, too, am quiet,
my usual joy tempered with the knowledge that this is the last
time life will be like this, that I will be getting ready for a prayer
meeting in this room my father built for us; the last time I will fan
the incense pot until the coals glow red and melt the grains of
Three Kings into a perfumed smoke that tickles my nose.

Members of our little prayer-group trickle in: my godmother,
with her razor wit and unusual sayings; my godfather, her
nephew, who sweeps me off my feet whenever he sees me no matter how much heavier I've gotten; Aunty Queen, who I convinced
with two-year-old sincerity that contrary to what Mom says, I
should have juice for breakfast instead of tea, our secret for the
years she took care of me; Reynold, her son, whose shy smile and
intriguing facial mole garnered a huge crush that lasted through
my adolescence; Uncle John, who always said, "Don't look at me
in that tone of voice," in his heavy baritone every time he made a
silly joke and we rolled our eyes; and other friends and well-wishers.

As they change into their gleaming white dresses and shirts, their chatter, their pleasantries wash over me, a familiar tide of words and laughter softening the silence.

We begin at nine sharp. The routine unfolds the same as other times, but today it is charged. We sing. Mom has chosen all my favorite hymns, and I sing them with gusto. I know all the words by heart so I can close my eyes to better feel the music that will carry me over the ocean, that will sing to me of home when I am no longer here. My godmother prays her quaint prayers, littered with language from another time, blessing the house, "the four corners and the binding center," and the children, "the lads and the damsels," but today her voice cracks as she prays "especially for that young damsel about to cross the brining ocean." Tears ooze through her sealed eyelids, meander down her weathered cheeks. When she is finished, my father helps her to stand, she sits next to me, squeezes my hand tightly.

My brother reads a psalm: "Bless the Lord O my soul all that is within me bless His holy name." It is, after all, a day of thanksgiving. Reynold, the intellectual, reads from the gospels. It is the story of the ten lepers healed by Christ, of whom only one turns back to give thanks; when he is finished, he gives his little homily. "To whom much is given," he says, looking straight at me, "much is expected." He goes on to speak of the importance of saying thank you, of gratitude.

And I am grateful. I am fortunate to embark on a journey that will take me to new and exciting places, one that will provide opportunities that I would not have had otherwise. I will go to college—the first in my family to do so, and I will make a life for myself and for those behind: my sister, my brother, my parents. Much has been given, much is expected, and suddenly I am afraid. For I know, too, that the bank has refused our loan, that the plane tickets have to be paid for, that all our savings have been converted and amount to less than 500 U.S. dollars. I know that my father is still not working; there are schoolbooks and uniforms to get for my brother and sister, and I am building my future at their expense.

They trust me to make their sacrifice worthwhile. And I know that I do not know this place I am going to, that I love what I am leaving behind. I am struck with terror.

My mother nudges me, passes me the candle—it is my turn to pray. I kneel in front of the chapel, and close my eyes, try to find that place where I can say the words—the usual "forgive our sins, give us grace, bless the world, bless the poor, bless the family, bless the studies"—but I cannot find it, I cannot pray. I feel my mother's glance, and she softly hums a hymn, giving me the time I need, the room follows her lead. I feel the weight of expectation bearing down. I feel my mother move, and hear the swish of breath as she blows the coals alive. The perfume of Three Kings tickles memory; the rising odor lifts the veil of darkness, and with it, the burden from my shoulders. I pray.

The Lord is my shepherd, I shall not want. He maketh me to lie down in green pastures. He leadeth me beside still waters, he restoreth my soul. He leadeth me in the paths of righteousness for his name's sake. Yea though I walk through the valley of the shadow of death, I shall fear no evil, for Thou art with me ... Surely Thy loving kindness and tender mercies shall follow me all the days of my life, and I shall dwell in the house of the Lord, forever.

The psalm is complete, but I find I cannot stop. The words keep tumbling, cascading from my lips. *I shall not want .... I shall fear no evil ... Thou art with me ... my cup shall be filled.* I say the words and pray them again and again needing to cling to that promise, needing to know that I will be all right. I stop, exhausted. I feel hands grasp mine, wrap around my waist, rest on my shoulders; they give me strength. I pray. Forgive our sins, give us grace, bless the world, bless the poor, bless the family, bless the studies, bless us all. Sign of the cross. I open my eyes. My mother is at my back, hands on my shoulders; my sister kneels behind her, arms wrapped around my waist, tears wetting my skirt waist. On either side is my godmother, and Aunty Queen, arthritis forgotten as they kneel holding the hands I had outstretched blindly. We are still for a moment. In the background, Uncle John begins to sing, something happy, something joyful, and slowly I rise. I help the others to their feet, swipe the back of my hand across my cheeks abashedly, and I too begin to sing. I feel light, unburdened, filled with a rush of joy. This was my dream; this was what I had always wanted. And I can come home to these people who love me enough to celebrate my success, even if it means I have to leave them.

My brother begins to clap in time and soon we are all singing at the top of our voices, clapping, making joyful noises. We end on a high note, with buoyant spirits and voracious appetites. My father fetches the fresh loaves of bread; the curry, the *rôti*, the platters of fried chicken and pots of *pelau* are unveiled and we bless the meal. We sit scattered around the house and I hoard the snippets of conversation, the laughter, the tidbits of well-meaning advice: "Now mind dem boys and dem eh!" "Doh travel late in de night, New York have all dem crazy people!" "Make sure yuh go to church on Sunday." "Enjoy yuhself, but doh forget what it is you gone to do!" I smile and nod, give the final farewell hugs and kisses. Smoke from the dying coals curls around the house, wraps itself in our hair and clothes. I will not forget this day, this covenant, this promise. I am filled with gratitude.

II.

July 17th, 1997

You get two suitcases, 70 pounds each—that's all. So you get the biggest ones you can find for the cheapest price you can, and even if they're the ugliest things you've ever seen you listen to your mother when she says it doesn't matter. So you pick the lesser eyesore, the plain black pseudo-leather, having decided that you absolutely could not live with the embroidered floral one, no matter how much easier it would be to spot on the carousel. Only one black one is left in the store, the attendant shrugs, so you wind up with one of each—fair compromise. For days they are stowed in the back of the house, out of sight, hidden as though the lineup of documents—tickets, passports, I-20, scholarship letters—the piles of books and shoes, the lists of things to do, things to get, things to remember tacked onto your bedroom wall, the mirror on your dresser and the refrigerator are not reminder enough that the day is approaching—you are leaving soon.

You've been preparing for days, running around doing laundry and quick shopping, gathering last-minute gifts from friends and family. You've held divorce court with your sister over which stuffed animals belong to whom (you decide to split them evenly based on a compromise between actual ownership and misplaced sentimental value). The warmest things owned by anybody remotely your size have crawled out from exile in storage boxes and mothballed dresser drawers to land on your sister's bed in a pile of long sleeves and collars, flannel, corduroy, and other thick, unnamable materials. Each item—the checkered blazer, the maroon shirt, the fuzzy blue bathrobe and the tan turtleneck—has a tale: "I had this when I went to Canada, (or England or New York or nowhere at all)." "I have no use for it now, so…It's too big for me anyway, and I thought…"

Because you share a room, your sister's bed becomes the hub of all this activity. She hasn't slept in it for over a week, and you have been fighting over who takes more than her fair share of covers as you huddle together in one bed, but neither of you sleep in the living room. In the mornings you wake up wrapped around each other. Some days you lie and listen to the hiss of her breath as she sleeps, feel the dead weight of her arm thrown across your stomach, her hands clutching your nightgown like a baby. You try to remember these moments during the spontaneous, all-out wars that seem to break out for trivial reasons between you during the day, that usually result in her stalking off in tears. When you express concern your mother says not to worry, that it will pass.

On the floor beside the bed are your books; you have many and have spent hours deliberating over which ones stay behind, which must be sent on later, which can be given away. You take none of your two hundred or so "trashy" romance novels—not even one to read on the plane—you have read them all already. You give away *Calabash Alley, Smile Orange*, and *A House for Mr. Biswas* (you especially *hated* the last one), and reluctantly agree to give your Enid Blyton, Nancy Drew, and Hardy Boy collections to your younger cousins. You feel a pang as you decide that your "good" books: *Shane, Wuthering Heights, The Chrysalids*, T.S. Eliot's *Collected Poems, Jane Eyre* can be sent on later, your old Chemistry and Physics texts and notebooks are more important—you do not know that you will later regret that decision, that you will wind up scribbling poems in margins and changing your Radiology major to English.

In another bundle are your going-away presents which keep growing in size and oddity: food, pens, books, cards, stationery, locally made jewelry, inspirational plaques, and funny little basket crafts. You are touched by the thoughts, but sometimes wonder what it was about you that could possibly indicate that you would like tie-dyed polyester blouses, earrings the color of the national flag, or a calabash purse—things you wouldn't be caught dead wearing under any circumstances. You feel mean-spirited and ungrateful, as you wonder why they didn't just give you the money— it would have been more than welcome and certainly easier to pack.

Pack. It is the night before you leave. The last of your visitors are gone and only the family remains: Mom, ready to get down to business, and Ray, willing to fetch and carry as instructed; Dad, in the kitchen preparing your favorite dinner—*dahl* with pig's tail and rice— avoiding business at all costs, and Debra, listless, trying to look cheerful and failing miserably. And you, certain that there is something you should be doing, but not quite sure what it is.

Aunty Marge is the travel expert who knows how to stuff underwear and socks into shoes, wrap packets of your favorite candy in your new sweaters, and how to roll t-shirts so they occupy less space. She doesn't know how to deal with the books though—

no one has ever needed to take such big ones or quite so many with them before. She talks non-stop about duty free shops, departure taxes, which lines to get into, how early to get to the airport, which shoes to wear, what not to tell the customs officers; about New York: how cheap everything is, how cold the winters are, how good the shopping is on Flatbush and Church Avenues. You try to tuck the facts away into exhausted brain cells.

The ugly suitcases are summoned, the smell of their newness unzipped into the purposeful air. They are laid open on your bedroom floor, two yawning, hungry holes in the center of your fuzzy brown carpet. You try to help appease their emptiness and walk back and forth with items as they are called for: "The other side of that shoe, that shirt—no, not that one, the other one!" You can't seem to get anything right, so you are brushed aside and you hover uselessly. Every now and again your aunt slips in a package of something or other that you are to deliver to a cousin, a friend, a person you never heard of. You try desperately not to resent the loss of precious space, console yourself with the fact that you can put some things into your mother's suitcase too, since she will accompany you for a short while. Eventually you are shooed away as Aunty Marge and Mom get down to the technicalities of stuffing and tucking. "Go help yuh father or get some rest, or something."

You are tired. It has been a hectic week of visits to family that you have not seen in years, old teachers and parish priests, the doctor, the dentist, the pharmacy. There were last minute get-togethers and lunches with friends from church, from school, from piano lessons, the last fêtes with your crew at Club Celebs and Upper Level. There was your own goodbye party, the first party you had ever been given, where your three best friends popped Stevie Wonder's "That's What Friends Are For" into your stereo and surrounded you in a nostalgic circle where you hugged each other and cried.

But you cannot go to sleep. You are looking at the knot of the mosquito net hanging above your bed, remembering how getting it just right across the bed baffled you as a child. You are breathing the smell of freshly turned soil and overripe fruit: Julie mangoes and cherries, passion fruit and guava, tomatoes and melangeone. You are looking outside into the darkness at the scenery that you have known all your life: the mango tree that you just knew housed a monster at five or six, that you could have kissed when you came home from surgery and a week in the hospital at thirteen, that always fascinated you because it looked like it was on fire in the sunset; the coconut tree that you watched your father climb, whose nuts were filled with sweet water, whose leaves you learned to make brooms and mats from, whose fruit you grated to make sweet bread, coconut bake, and sugar cake.

You walk around, look at the marks on your wall where you tried to grow by measuring your height at least three times a day; see the black smudge behind the bed head where you scribbled "Lauren and Troy forever" and later tried to erase it. You run your fingers along the sticker collection you and your brother labored over for years, remembering how diligent you were at buying candy every day just for the stickers inside, smile at the pride you felt in knowing exactly how many were pasted across the wooden beam.

You think, too, of your red dress, your favorite dingy white t-shirts and your comfortable, if bummy "home clothes" still folded on your shelf, that you've been told have no place in a new life. You turn around just as your mother is about to toss out your favorite nightie (the pink flowered one with the white bow on the neck and the hole on the shoulder) and you scream "NO!" maybe a little louder than you intended. Her hand freezes mid-air and there is a heartbeat of silence. Aunty Marge protests, "But the weight—you only get 70 pounds!" But your mother looks at you and says, "We'll make room."

III.

July 18th, 1997

At seven-thirty A.M., a small pickup truck barrels down the almost-

52

deserted Southern Main Road; the rustling green stalks of the cane fields and the clear blueness of the sky whiz by in an indistinguishable blur of color and quiet. At traffic-light stops, it is possible to detect the signs of stirring: taxi drivers pulling into the stands; one or two lone travelers waiting roadside, flagging cars that pass by; the sounds of "mornin' neighbor" across fences, cocoyea brooms sweeping yards, and the creak of rusty gates as early-bird stores open for business.

The driver sits with one arm slung out of the window, the other gripping the steering wheel, his jaw tense and his brow furrowed in concentration. In the passenger seats are the mother, who leans against the headrest, paying half-attention to her aunt, Marge, whose hands move constantly to keep pace with her story, most of which is lost to the wind as it whips through the open window.

In the truck's covered tray are two large suitcases: one black and the other a hodge-podge of colors set with large white flowers, both adorned with red dancing strips of fabric tied to the handles. Beside them lie a less imposing heap of backpacks and pocketbooks, another smaller suitcase, and a duffle bag, most of which also wear the red fabric. An odd assortment of four people sit precariously on the none-too-sturdy boards that serve as benches, lined along the side of the truck. A wiry boy of seventeen chatters incessantly, addressing an animated stream of commentary to his father, a man with a placid expression who responds with an occasional nod or rumble. On the right sit two girls; the taller is almost folded in two, her knees high up to her chest. She wears a baseball cap pulled low over her eyes and does not face the rest of the group, her back turned slightly and her head resting against the window facing the cab. She is silent, observing the others from beneath the dark shadow of the New York Yankees and rolls her eyes every now and then at some question or statement issued by her brother or father across the suitcases.

But the other girl is most interesting; the voices and the silences seem to center around her. She sits facing the open back of the truck, her feet just hanging over the edge, her hands gripping the side to steady herself against the jouncing motion. Her dark slacks, long-sleeved shirt and jacket contrast sharply with the little brown truck and the casual tee-shirts and jeans of the others. Her eyes alternate between a wild darting, as if trying to suck up the whirl of the passing landscape, and vacancy as her gaze clouds over and her eyelids begin to droop. At one point, her eyes fall shut and her hands loosen their hold and her body leans a little too far over the edge of the truck. Her father calls her name sharply and swiftly grabs her jacket. She jerks awake, but shrugs off his arm.

After a while, the houses, thick bushes and lush trees begin to thin into the flat plains of the airport, where the truck finally passes a sign saying "Piarco International Airport next left." Soon, they pull in front of a drab, unimposing building and stop. The mother turns to tap on the glass, nodding and making "We're here!" gestures. After a brief moment of stillness, everyone jumps into action. Aunty Marge commandeers a cart as the van driver, the boy, and his father unload the luggage. The girl hops out, absently straightens her clothes and hair; her sister emerges reluctantly, jumping to the ground and stretching her long arms into the air.

The younger woman is agitated at the long lines at the check-in counter. "Marge, I knew we should have come here earlier!" she fusses to the older woman, who is unperturbed and working her way to the shortest line. "Annette, stop fretting," she replies, directing the others to take places in the other two lines, "Whoever gets through first, call us." She turns to the girl in the jacket, "Yuh have the tickets? The passports?" As the requested documents are produced, she nods her head approvingly. The lines move slowly, but eventually the boy waves as he reaches the check-in counter farthest to the left. The others abandon their posts and move toward him, ignoring the displeased look of the other passengers.

The agent checks the two passports and as the suitcases are loaded onto the scale, the two women look at each other and cross their fingers. 69.5…65…80…76. "These two are overweight," the agent says, stating the obvious. "Is those books," Marge hisses, maneuvering her way to the counter. "Miss, hear dis, she get a scholarship an' she goin' away to school in New York. She had to take all her books and we tried to keep in the limit, but they was so heavy, and she had to take clothes an' ting too, yuh know…" The agent is unimpressed, but looks at the winding line behind them, nods and attaches the labels to the luggage. The group breathes a collective sigh of relief and shuffles into the lobby.

"Well, I guess this is it," the father intones, chest puffed out, a sure indication that a long speech is about to follow. He is cut off by a muffled cry as the taller girl strides off, pulling her cap lower onto her face. Marge moves toward her, but the girl in the jacket intervenes, "I'll get it." Her sister turns away at the sound of the approaching footsteps. "Hey," says the girl in the jacket, touching her gently on the shoulder, pretending not to hear the stifled sobs. No response. A moment of silence. "Don't go." The two words float between the girls for an eternity. "I have to." Another moment of silence. "Fine then, go." Swiping her eyes, she turns and walks back toward the group. The mother tugs her closer by the bill of her Yankees cap and kisses her atop her head. The girl resists, then succumbs, wrapping her arms tightly around her mother.

At the gate a flurry of hugs and kisses ensue—Aunty Marge still giving advice: "Make sure yuh go in the right line when yuh reach!" The mother giving last minute instructions to the other three, "Dennis, you have the number in New York if there are any prob-lems—and don't forget the light bill. You two, don't give your father any trouble, especially you eh Debra…and Ray, take care of your sister until I get back. Be good!" The girl in the jacket gives everyone a final embrace, then stands apart, hiking her backpack higher on her back. "Are you ready?" her mother asks. She nods. They show their tickets and go through, waving as they wait for their bags to be scanned. "We'll be in the waving gallery!" the boy shouts.

Mother and daughter do not speak as they pay their departure tax and walk around trying to find the right gate and arrive just as the plane is beginning to be boarded. The gate attendant issues their passes and directs them down the narrow stairs and out of the building toward the aircraft. As they walk the girl feels the heels of her shoes sinking into the asphalt, already growing soft in the early heat. She yanks each footstep out and continues to move forward, eyeing the parked plane like a finish line. She imagines the trail of prints she must be leaving in her wake, but does not look, afraid she might be tempted to follow them back, afraid she would turn, like Lot's wife, into a pillar of salt. The mother pokes the girl and points to the waving gallery, shielding her eyes with one hand. "Can you see them?" The girl remarks that it is too far away and besides there is a glare on the glass. Her mother does not hear because she is busy flapping her arms at the nebulous mass of gesticulating people in the distance, all focused on the line of travelers making their way to the plane.

They climb the narrow stairs, find their places and stow their belongings. The girl sighs deeply, a long, relieved rush of breath, and nestles into her window seat. Her mother too, pauses, leans into the headrest, eyes shut and whispers, "Thank you Father, we made it." The plane engine hums accompaniment to the murmur of passengers settling in: the scratch of fabric, newspapers rustling, the tick-tocks of the flight attendants' heels, the determined snaps of overhead compartments.

A voice comes over the intercom—"Thank you for flying BWIA, this is your captain speaking and we will soon be departing for John F. Kennedy International Airport in New York. Our estimated time of arrival is…" and fades as the plane readies for takeoff. The mother jumps up excitedly and peers over the girl's lap as the plane begins to turn, squinting through the window, still waving. Over her shoulder she asks, "Lauren, aren't you going to say goodbye? This is the last…" she trails off and shakes her head in disbelief. The girl is asleep.

IV.

September 2nd, 1997

My mother returns home this morning. "Take care, love, and be

56

good!" she whispers in my ear as she hugs me tight, then disappears through the gate. We have an agreement: no crying, no mushy stuff. And so we both continue to wave, huge smiles plastered across our faces, each pretending not to see the shimmer of restrained tears in the other's eyes. Her bags come through on the other side of the scanner and for a moment she is distracted, gathering them, tucking the large bear we purchased for my sister under her arm.

This is the day that I have been longing for, a day I pictured a thousand times those long nights of penning letters to schools, asking for a chance; the day I planned and re-planned since the moment I found out about my scholarship. And here it is. In a few minutes, I will officially be living in New York on my own. No Mom, no Dad, just me and my new life. I will make my pilgrimage to the city, walk in places I have seen only on television, created in my dreams: subways, The World Trade Center, Broadway, The Empire State Building, Brooklyn, Central Park, Times Square; I will delve headfirst into the magic of the world's most exciting city. I am ready, and have been guiltily counting the days until Mum's worrying watchfulness would board the plane back to Trinidad.

Yet the moment I can no longer see my mother's face, I want to run—past the security guards and their metal detectors, past the queue of impatient passengers—as fast as my legs can carry me. I want to run, throw myself into her arms and beg her not to leave me in this alien place—to take me home. My muscles tighten in response to the surge of adrenaline: fight or flight. My mother turns around just then and our eyes met. Her gaze reassures me, calms the furious throbbing in my chest, the utterance rising in my throat—I will be fine. She twists the bear and makes it do a goofy wave with its furry paw; I roll my eyes and smile. "I love you," she mouths, as she blows a kiss at me, turns and walks away briskly. I look at her receding back, ramrod straight as always and I know that she is not going to look back. I turn toward the exit, and begin my journey to the place I will call home.

LINDA PARSONS MARION

WANDERLUST

for Rachel

A swat of the Welsh wind scuttled you
down the Swansea coast, already the world
traveler. In London hostels you lived on
tins of beans and tomatoes, one eye peeled
for mice and punk thieves. That summer
you shared a flat with New Zealanders above
the chocolate shoppe, arranged lemon tarts
in their paper buntings for the festival goers,
Edinburgh's midnight sun playing brilliantly on.

You'll return to Tennessee foothills
arched and licking your ankles, though soon
you'll tire of it all—this insignificant house,
nursery rocker in the attic stained with hours
we sailed hungering under the cheddar moon,
friends whose folded pictures you carried
on the Tube, hometown baggage a sinker's
weight luring little worth remembering.

In my mind, you say, I'm *over there*.
Maybe you'll move to New York or Charleston,
someplace not Knoxville, not *here*.
Just when your heels settle into purple phlox
and the lilacs ripen, when *home* thrums
a steady, almost forgotten rain, the far
distance opens its heaven.

Born under the fierce bull, sign you will
go where you will, child of cities and rural
parts, daughter of cobbled and crooked streets.
With no one to warn you of lake's shoulder,

alley, uncovered well, journey homeroads
until time to set out. Until then, pack light,
intent on the song of here and there,
the rough seeds of becoming
tucked under your tongue.

DIANE GILLIAM

CRESCENDO, DECRESCENDO

Between coughing fits that are lasting,
tonight, ten to fifteen minutes,
my daughter is playing her violin.
She's sixteen, back in her room because
she doesn't like me to watch her cough.
I'm in the living room reading
but when she coughs I stop
like when I was a little girl playing statues
and to win I held myself still
and thought I wasn't allowed to breathe.

Now her violin draws a long, quivering
breath, lets it out slowly
without catching. She pulls the notes
like long, silky filament
drawn smooth and whole from a rough
snarl of frayed, splintery stuff.
The note climbs then cracks
and collapses when the cough
comes back. It is a sound
like your house being torn down.

I can't help it, I take a deep breath,
head down the hallway to her room.
Before I get to her door, the violin
stutters and begins to cry which means
at least she is breathing and I
begin to cry, like when she was born,
when they said she could breathe on her own
so they went ahead and cut the cord.

DEDE WILSON

THE LOCK

A key in the lock, the sound,
    Returns my roving daughter.
She's home. She's safe. She's found.
A key in the lock, the sound
Spins me right around.
    How gaily she would enter!
A key in the lock, the sound,
    Returns my roving daughter.

A step, a voice in the hall,
    The gladness of her laughter.
Wait! I hear footfalls,
A step, a voice in the hall—
But it's not her at all.
    No happily, ever, after.
A step, a voice in the hall,
    The gladness of her laughter.

The sound of the door: the click,
    The hush, the lock, the hollow
Sound it encloses. *Scrit*
Goes the lock, and the clock tick-ticks
The sound of the door, the click
    When it closes. Whose footsteps follow
The sound of the door—the click,
    The hush, the lock, the hollow?

REBECCA MCCLANAHAN

DEMETER, GODDESS OF EARTH
(from "THE SEVEN WIVES OF ZEUS")

My life did not begin
with his touch, nor with the mortal Iasion,
though we lay together in a thrice-plowed
field till Zeus, passing in a cloud,
saw us there and wanted that heat.
Secretly every man wants a woman with dirt
on her hands, a woman bent over a plow,
sowing the empty furrow.
Yes, Zeus was lusty, nearly my match.
Together from our thrones we would watch
the flocks below as they drifted
on the hills, till bored with godliness, we shifted
shapes, I a mare and he a bull.
We were both at home in the animal.
I might have stayed there always, the corn goddess
stripped willingly of her crown, barley princess
forever young. I did not know the seed
of a daughter would sprout and feed
that hollow place. But from our union
Kore was born and Love opened its thousand
blossoms. From that day on
I was Mother and life began.
And Zeus who knew all, knew that. One
nod to his brother Hades and she was gone,
sucked to the world below where Kore
became Persephone,
wife of darkness. You know the rest.
You call it a happy ending, the daughter lost
now found, how Zeus finally gave in

to my cries so the dying earth would live again.
But to me there is no victory
when every autumn I lose her to a husband, bury
my treasure in the ground,
the same soil where once I found
my life in *her*. When you've lost your daughter,
what does it matter that the whole earth calls you Mother.

BETTY ADCOCK

MOTHER TO DAUGHTER, 19

You are a darkness tensed
in an egg-pale house. It is
fragile as a plash of spotlight.
Blackbird,
                you sit. Black pearl,
you roll in place.
Rocking toward edges, you wait.
Light that I cast was around you and window.
Now this.

When your eyes have broken open,
when your mouth can utter the knowledge
that's starless, I will keep
under my own lids
a confetti of morning,
something to wish on.

What will you eat, my darling?
What will you dance, awake
in the gutter and smoke of the gone
day that was our one candle?

For now, you're the black backing
the mirror—can I bear my own reflection?
the family photographs coming clear to you
only in the darkness behind things.
Will we know one another there?

When you wake to the self
dark and world dark, the real
night you have slept through, to find
the whole astounding circumference kin,

you will cry out
Mother! Ashes!

And bright as any tiger, any sun,
your light will begin to burn.

—1978

BETTY ADCOCK

A TRUE STORY

I have not looked at "Mother to Daughter, 19" for many years. I have never published it anywhere. It is one of those poems written out of necessity, late at night, riddled with deep emotion; one of those poems that seems to be simply a kind of cry.

The date on the poem reveals how long ago the necessary great separation took place between my daughter and me. Of course it would take another story, years later, to tell how we came together again, and how well we get along, how much I admire her work (she is a fine journalist) and how thoughtful she is toward me and her father, how independent she is.

That said, I can go back to the night I wrote this poem, revised almost not at all. I was completely unprepared, foolishly so, for the inevitable conflicts, the lashing out at me, the unexplained hostility of a young girl needing to be cut loose. She wanted everything, suddenly. She wanted even her own suffering. She was an only child, part of the problem of course; and we had been, I thought, very close. Suddenly she became someone I didn't know at all.

I knew, intellectually, that all this had to come. Emotionally I was undone by it. My own mother had died when I was barely six years old. My father never remarried. An only child myself, I grew up in a huge Victorian house with grandparents, a great aunt, my father, an uncle by marriage and the aunt who reared me. There were no cousins to play with. My aunt was an extremely narrow person, well-meaning but unable to show affection and sometimes given to mean manipulation of the child in her care. The narrative of my childhood—and perhaps of my life itself—is the narrative of the lost mother, the story of *Mother-in-Heaven* waiting for me, the story of my longing. And one important thread of that story was the fact that my aunt was not my mother, and therefore I could put a kind of shield around myself. I didn't have to love her, and I didn't. My childhood was wonderful in many ways, because

66

there was the extended family in the house, and woods and fields to roam in, and plenty of imaginary journeys. But it was awful in the loss that was somehow the linchpin of my life.

And so I did not have to break away from my aunt, or anyone. I was never really connected to her but rather to an idealized figure of the vanished real mother—who of course exacted nothing from me and created no conflicts of interests!

Therefore, when my sweet, wonderful daughter began to chew off the umbilical cord, as it were, beginning her necessary breakaway, I very nearly went down for the count. I had had absolutely no experience of what was happening. The result was a couple of very hard years in which nothing my daughter said was understood and nothing I said was understood. We just wandered around in the dark bumping into each other. I was terrified for her during that time, very afraid of what she might do to damage her life, her possibilities. I was terrified of her as well, for she had huge power over me.

I think my own turning point came when I was hiking one morning on a wild forest trail alone. I sat on a log in a gorgeous spot I knew well, tall hardwoods all around, one of those places where the horizon-hum of our machines is stilled and we can hear everything at the edge of silence—one leaf striking earth, the lightest breeze, an animal's footfall, all the intricate conversations of October. I was trying for balance, for the wisdom to know what, if anything, I should do. Maybe it was here, where the sun could ignite a single leaf to ruby brilliance and the world could be simple and palpable and sane. In a moment of reckless meditation, I found myself creating a little ritual, the way I had sometimes done as a child—I had once buried my real ruby ring among oak roots in such a moment. Now, in an autumn forest far from my child-hood, I gave up something else.

I gave my daughter to the trees.

I spent the morning offering her up to the earth's beauty and necessity; to her own trail hacked out herself; to what is lovely, harsh, and mother to us all in this creature-crowded green heaven that is the real world (when we can find it). Always something of a pantheist, I came every morning for many weeks to this place, this mothering place, to offer my daughter to the trees.

Crazy? Maybe.

But was it a coincidence that two years later my daughter would walk with me to that very spot deep in the woods—her own idea for a special celebration of my forty-third birthday. Of course she had no notion that she'd been placed in the keeping of those very oaks and hickories. That birthday is likely my most cherished memory as a mother. Still in college, having no extra money to buy presents, my daughter promised a surprise as she drove me out to the country. She led me along the favored trail, the one we'd hiked together when she was younger, the one I'd followed alone to equilibrium on all those mornings during the time of our near-estrangement. We came to the heavily wooded area, the log to sit on, and she presented her gift: a story. Her literature class had just studied "A White Heron" by Sarah Orne Jewett, a writer whose work was just being rediscovered. My beautiful daughter sat in the dappled sun filtering through the branches and read aloud to me Jewett's lovely century-old tale of solitude and contradictory feelings and unconditional love for the wild world. Just that: a story read aloud on a September afternoon. The best gift I ever had, and one which seemed to verify my probably absurd belief that, under the calm of those trees, I could somehow find what to do, and what not to do, in order to let my daughter go in confidence that she could find her way without harm.

And of course we have disagreed and fought and hurt each other since. But we have never again had that near-total loss of one another that was, I now think, inevitable—just as its ending was inevitable.

Now there are granddaughters: two wonderful girls, ages seven and three, that Sylvia and her husband adopted from China. And yes, my daughter has the same name as the girl in Jewett's story, and it was the name of the mother I lost so early in my life. Watching Sylvia caring for Tai and Mollie, I see such a lively happiness, such a living mothering, I feel myself freed from my old longing into pure delight. We freed each other, my Sylvia and I.

I do not know if this poem, written in the saddest part of our struggle to recreate our relationship, is good poetry. It is filled with the darkness of my foreboding and fear, the darkness of her refusal and need, and with the darkness of isolation we both experienced. But this darkness, part of growing up, part of letting someone grow up, is also the dark in which "family photographs" become clear, in which we begin to know one another and create our own light. The poem was written at a crossroads of terror, hurt, fear, change, my own childhood haunting—a crossroads of past and future. Yet the last two lines show how, even then, I knew that Sylvia would find her way into her own life and joy, and back into my own life as joy.

BETTY ADCOCK

To Sylvia, Grown Daughter

You who loved so much the creek mud
and the green-shaded woods, all many-
legged moving things, all small hiding
flowers—so like yourself then—
now you are this tall someone
and bright as a fire. Dear lantern!
But listen:

lit with fallen apples and plain grass,
with salamander and birdfeather,
with candles of spring pine,
the old rooms will have waited
the way a forgotten house waits at the edge
of a snapshot you hardly meant to take.
The place has its own moon
and no noise but the cricket's skinny one.

You may enter by the door of what is not yet,
as you did before. Or by the new door
of what has been taken from you.
Pain will let you in, or fury. Ordinary
love will let you in, or any dying.
No key is too odd, no reason too far away.

It is only the house of your first name
that belongs also to the skyful of branches,
to dove, treefrog, and milkweed,
those who begin again,
I say this because it is so simple.
I tell you because it is anyone's.
And because the likeness may be torn
by now, and you may not know.

BRENDA HILLMAN

BAND PRACTICE

—I dropped her off, she was balancing the guitar case
on her head, there was one of those abnormal green
            ladybugs on the front seat; I said:
    call me anyway even if you're happy—

MARILYN KALLET

Missing Heather

I kissed her goodbye
as she slept
(I should be shot
for leaving her)
but just as I was
pulling out of the drive
she rushed outside
in her tee-shirt
nightshirt
pale and sleep-
ridden
barefoot on
the gravel and
gave me a hug
I should say
she put her arms
down and
let herself be hugged
at thirteen
coolness is
everything
even if it's early
and only God is watching.

Hours later
in the San Francisco
airport I'm
frantic looking
for stamps
she'll think
as soon as the plane

took off
I'd forgotten her
now she won't even get
a letter from me at camp
(my mother would never
have run off
and left me to write
fershoogener poetry).

These last three months
I've done nothing but
prepare the house
for her Bat Mitzvah
done nothing but
complain about it
a hostile Yiddish Martha Stewart.

Now I miss my baby
I'm aching for her
like a wounded
lover

as if
she's the one
        leaving me

and I'm a ghost mother
with only word babies
waiting.

KATHRYN STRIPLING BYER

CHICAGO BOUND

On the day you turn twenty-one,
we arrive at the airport,
plenty of time before take-off,
the rain steady, ugly gray
sky while the radio cheers us

on, Jimmy Rogers and *Sweet Home
Chicago* just what we need on
this Friday you turn twenty-one.
Come on, come on, let's get a move on.
I'm ready, Daddy, to leave this town.

I hold my breath while the plane rises,
muddy clouds all the way up
till we come out the other side into
the stratosphere, lapis lazuli and white
shag carpet all the way there.

Nobody at home up here. Makes me
feel lonesome till I see the beverage cart
rolling toward us and lower my tray.
What's for lunch? Nothing much.
Cookie, sandwich, a small Baby Ruth.

Captain's voice from the cockpit
keeps telling us how long before
we'll come down. Soon it's time for a snooze
while this plane flies us over the heartland
to you in your Shakespeare class,

old boss man Lear raving blank verse,
still crazy after all these years. Just a little while
longer, we'll be on the ground

where we'll hop a train south to the campus,
a place I like better than this flimsy

carpet of clouds on which I cannot walk
to you. I need green fields
to do that, some tough city blocks,
Kimbark, Ellis, East Hyde Park.
Give me boulevard, avenue,

chemin, rue, strasse, calle,
avenida, el camino, whatever
you want to call it, Baby, if it's down
there on earth where you are,
it's Sweet Home. I'll take it.

Kathryn Stripling Byer, Corinna Lynette Byer, and Arjun

II. Hello, Mother, Goodbye

SHARON OLDS

THE SOUND

The morning our daughter has come home, I hear
a sound, over my head—like angels,
or the pinging in my ears, sometimes,
in bed, or the noise of a planet's ring,
the whir of dry grit around it.
It comes and goes, a cosmic zinging,
finally I realize it's a woman singing,
actually a woman humming
in the room above me—it's our girl, unpacking—
the floor boards creak, I hear it and then don't,
as if a wind carries it unevenly,
clear, high, casual, watery humming.
It sounds like a summer band at a distance,
or music made with the back of the mind,
purposeless, melodious chaff of a
woman puttering, her soprano saying
Here is no harm, we improvise
on the edge of milk and sleep. And it's
so intimate, without witness,
as if I were hearing the workings of her muscles
as she lifts and unfolds, each garment doubles,
quadruples like the zygote. I have never, before, heard a
grown woman singing alone—
my mother mostly yoo-hooed to a male
God, gorgeously screamed for help—
now, below our daughter's crooning,
I lean, here, like a newborn freshly
arrived in a home, or an embryo
in the belly of a woman whom homecoming has made
musical, the body's harmony
audible, as if matter itself were merciful.

JAMAICA KINCAID

THE CIRCLING HAND

D uring my holidays from school, I was allowed to stay in bed until long after my father had gone to work. He left our house every weekday at the stroke of seven by the Anglican church bell. I would lie in bed awake, and I could hear all the sounds my parents made as they prepared for the day ahead. As my mother made my father his breakfast, my father would shave, using his shaving brush that had an ivory handle and a razor that matched, then he would step outside to the little shed he had built for us as a bathroom, to quickly bathe in water that he had instructed my mother to leave outside overnight in the dew. That way, the water would be very cold, and he believed that cold water strengthened his back. If I had been a boy, I would have gotten the same treatment, but since I was a girl, and on top of that went to school only with other girls, my mother would always add some hot water to my bathwater to take off the chill. On Sunday afternoons, while I was in Sunday school, my father took a hot bath, the tub was half-filled with plain water, and then my mother would add a large caldronful of water in which she had just boiled some bark and leaves from a bay-leaf tree. The bark and leaves were there for no reason other than that he liked the smell. He would then spend hours lying in this bath, studying his pool coupons or drawing examples of pieces of furniture he planned to make. When I came home from Sunday school, we would sit down to Sunday dinner.

My mother and I often took a bath together. Sometimes it was just a plain bath, which didn't take very long. Other times, it was a special bath in which the barks and flowers of many different trees, together with all sorts of oils, were boiled in the same large caldron. We would then sit in this bath in a darkened room with a strange-smelling candle burning away. As we sat in this bath, my mother would bathe different parts of my body, then she would do the same to herself. We took these baths after my mother had consulted with her obeah woman, and with her mother and a trusted friend, and all three of them had confirmed that from the look of things around our house—the way a small scratch on my instep had turned into a small sore, then a large sore, and how long it had taken to heal, the way a dog she knew, and a friendly dog at that, suddenly turned and bit her, how a porcelain bowl she had carried from one eternity and hoped to carry into the next suddenly slipped out of her capable hands and broke into pieces the size of grains of sand, how words she spoke in jest to a friend had been completely misunderstood—one of the many women my father had loved, had never married, but with whom he had had children was trying to harm my mother and me by setting bad spirits on us.

When I got up, I placed my bedclothes and my nightie in the sun to air out, brushed my teeth, and washed and dressed myself. My mother would then give me breakfast, but since, during my holidays, I was not going to school, I wasn't forced to eat an enormous breakfast of porridge, eggs, an orange or half a grapefruit, bread and butter, and cheese. I could get away with just some bread and butter and cheese and porridge and cocoa. I spent the day following my mother around and observing the way she did everything. When we went to the grocer's, she would point out to me the reason she bought each thing. I was shown a loaf of bread or a pound of butter from at least ten different angles. When we went to market, if that day she wanted to buy some crabs she would inquire from the person selling them if they came from near Parham, and if the person said yes my mother did not buy the crabs. In Parham was the leper colony, and my mother was convinced that the crabs ate nothing but the food from the lepers' own plates. If we were then to eat the crabs, it wouldn't be long before we were lepers ourselves and living unhappily in the leper colony.

How important I felt to be with my mother. For many people, their wares and provisions laid out in front of them, would brighten up when they saw her coming and would try hard to get her attention. They would dive underneath their stalls and bring out goods even better than what they had on display. They were disappointed when she held something up in the air, looked at it, turning it this way and that, and then, screwing up her face, said, "I don't think so," and turned and walked away—off to another stall to see if someone who only last week had sold her some delicious christophine had something that was just as good. They would call out after her turned back that next week they expected to have eddoes or dasheen or whatever, and my mother would say, "We'll see," in a very disbelieving tone of voice. If then we went to Mr. Kenneth, it would be only for a few minutes, for he knew exactly what my mother wanted and always had it ready for her. Mr. Kenneth had known me since I was a small child, and he would always remind me of little things I had done then as he fed me a piece of raw liver he had set aside for me. It was one of the few things I liked to eat, and, to boot, it pleased my mother to see me eat something that was so good for me, and she would tell me in great detail the effect the raw liver would have on my red blood corpuscles.

We walked home in the hot midmorning sun mostly without event. When I was much smaller, quite a few times while I was walking with my mother she would suddenly grab me and wrap me up in her skirt and drag me along with her as if in a great hurry. I would hear an angry voice saying angry things, and then, after we had passed the angry voice, my mother would release me. Neither my mother nor my father ever came straight out and told me anything, but I had put two and two together and I knew that it was one of the women that my father had loved and with whom he had had a child or children, and who never forgave him for marrying my mother and having me. It was one of those women who were always trying to harm my mother and me, and they must have loved my father very much, for not once did any of them ever try to hurt him, and whenever he passed them on the street it was as if he and these women had never met.

When we got home, my mother started to prepare our lunch

(pumpkin soup with droppers, banana fritters with salt fish stewed in antroba and tomatoes, fungi with salt fish stewed in antroba and tomatoes, or pepper pot, all depending on what my mother had found at market that day). As my mother went about from pot to pot, stirring one, adding something to the other, I was ever in her wake. As she dipped into a pot of boiling something or other to taste for correct seasoning, she would give me a taste of it also, asking me what I thought. Not that she really wanted to know what I thought, for she had told me many times that my taste buds were not quite developed yet, but it was just to include me in everything. While she made our lunch, she would also keep an eye on her washing. If it was a Tuesday and the colored clothes had been starched, as she placed them on the line I would follow, carrying a basket of clothespins for her. While the starched colored clothes were being dried on the line, the white clothes were being whitened on the stone heap. It was a beautiful stone heap that my father had made for her: an enormous circle of stones, about six inches high, in the middle of our yard. On it the soapy white clothes were spread out; as the sun dried them, bleaching out all stains, they had to be made wet again by dousing them with buckets of water. On my holidays, I did this for my mother. As I watered the clothes, she would come up behind me, instructing me to get the clothes thoroughly wet, showing me a shirt that I should turn over so that the sleeves were exposed

Over our lunch, my mother and father talked to each other about the houses my father had to build; how disgusted he had become with one of his apprentices, or with Mr. Oatie; what they thought of my schooling so far; what they thought of the noises Mr. Jarvis and his friends made for so many days when they locked themselves up inside Mr. Jarvis's house and drank rum and ate fish they caught themselves and danced to the music of an accordion that they took turns playing. On and on they talked. As they talked, my head would move from side to side, looking at them. When my eyes rested on my father, I didn't think very much of the way he looked. But when my eyes rested on my mother, I found her beautiful. Her head looked as if it should be on a sixpence. What a beautiful long neck, and long plaited hair, which she pinned up around the crown of her head because when her hair hung down it made her too hot. Her nose was the shape of a flower on the brink of opening. Her mouth, moving up and down as she ate and talked at the same time, was such a beautiful mouth I could have looked at it forever if I had to and not mind. Her lips were wide and almost thin, and when she said certain words I could see small parts of big white teeth—so big, and pearly, like some nice buttons on one of my dresses. I didn't much care about what she said when she was in this mood with my father. She made him laugh so. She could hardly say a word before he would burst out laughing. We ate our food, I cleared the table, we said goodbye to my father as he went back to work, I helped my mother with the dishes, and then we settled into the afternoon.

When my mother, at sixteen, after quarreling with her father, left his house on Dominica and came to Antigua, she packed all her things in an enormous wooden trunk that she had bought in Roseau for almost six shillings. She painted the trunk yellow and green outside, and she lined the inside with wallpaper that had a cream background with pink roses printed all over it. Two days after she left her father's house, she boarded a boat and sailed for Antigua. It was a small boat, and the trip would have taken a day and a half ordinarily, but a hurricane blew up and the boat was lost at sea for almost five days. By the time it got to Antigua, the boat was practically in splinters, and though two or three of the passengers were lost overboard, along with some of the cargo, my mother and her trunk were safe. Now, twenty-four years later, this trunk was kept under my bed, and in it were things that had belonged to me, starting from just before I was born. There was the chemise, made of white cotton, with scallop edging around the sleeves, neck, and hem, and white flowers embroidered on the front—the first garment I wore after being born. My mother had made them herself, and once, when we were passing by, I was even shown the tree under which she sat as she made this garment. There were some of my diapers, with their handkerchief hemstitch that she had also done herself; there was a pair of white wool booties with matching jacket and hat; there was a blanket in white wool and a blanket in white flannel cotton; there was a plain white linen hat with lace trimming; there was my christening outfit; there were two of my baby bottles: one in the shape of a normal baby bottle, and the other shaped like a boat, with a nipple on either end; there was a thermos in which my mother had kept a tea that was supposed to have a soothing effect on me; there was the dress I wore on my first birthday: a yellow cotton with green smocking on the front; there was the dress I wore on my second birthday: pink cotton with green smocking on the front; there was also a photograph of me on my second birthday wearing my pink dress and my first pair of earrings, a chain around my neck, and a pair of bracelets, all specially made of gold from British Guiana; there was the first pair of shoes I grew out of after I knew how to walk; there was the dress I wore when I first went to school, and the first notebook in which I wrote; there were the sheets for my crib and the sheets for my first bed; there was my first straw hat, my first straw basket—decorated with flowers—my grandmother had sent me from Dominica; there were my report cards, my certificates of merit from school, and my certificates of merit from Sunday school.

From time to time, my mother would fix on a certain place in our house and give it a good cleaning. If I was at home when she happened to do this, I was at her side, as usual. When she did this with the trunk, it was a tremendous pleasure, for after she had removed all the things from the trunk, and aired them out, and changed the camphor balls, and then refolded the things and put them back in their places in the trunk, as she held each thing in her hand she would tell me a story about myself. Sometimes I knew the story first hand, for I could remember the incident quite well; sometimes what she told me had happened when I was too young to know anything; and sometimes it happened before I was even born. Whichever way, I knew exactly what she would say, for I had heard it so many times before, but I never got tired of it. For instance, the flowers on the chemise, the first garment I wore after being born, were not put on correctly, and that is because when my mother was embroidering them I kicked so much that her hand was unsteady. My mother said that usually when I kicked around in her stomach and she told me to stop I would, but on that day I paid no attention at all. When she told me this story, she would smile at me and say, "You see, even them you were hard to manage." It pleased me to think that, before she could see my face, my mother spoke to me in the same way she did now. On and on my mother would go. No small part of my life was so unimportant that she hadn't made a note of it, and now she would tell it to me over and over again. I would sit next to her and she would show me the very dress I wore on the day I bit another child my age with whom I was playing. "Your biting phase," she called it. Or the day she warned me not to play around the coal pot, because I liked to sing to myself and dance around the fire. Two seconds later, I fell into the hot coals, burning my elbows. My mother cried when she saw that it wasn't serious, and now, as she told me about it, she would kiss the little black patches of scars on my elbows.

As she told me the stories, I sometimes sat at her side, leaning against her, or I would crouch on my knees behind her back and lean over her shoulder. As I did this, I would occasionally sniff at her neck, or behind her ears, or at her hair. She smelled sometimes of lemons, sometimes of sage, sometimes of roses, sometimes of bay leaf. At times I would no longer hear what it was she was saying; I just liked to look at her mouth as it opened and closed over words, or as she laughed. How terrible it must be for all the people who had no one to love them so and no one whom they loved so, I thought. My father, for instance. When he was a little boy, his parents, after kissing him goodbye and leaving him with his grandmother, boarded a boat and sailed to South America. He never saw them again, though they wrote to him and sent him presents—packages of clothes on his birthday and at Christmas.

He then grew to love his grandmother, and she loved him, for she took care of him and worked hard at keeping him well fed and clothed. From the beginning, they slept in the same bed, and as he became a young man they continued to do so. When he was no longer in school and had started working, every night, after he and his grandmother had eaten their dinner, my father would go off to visit his friends. He would then return home at around midnight and fall asleep next to his grandmother. In the morning, his grandmother would awake at half past five or so, a half hour before my father, and prepare his bath and breakfast and make everything proper and ready for him, so that at seven o'clock sharp he stepped out the door off to work. One morning, though, he overslept, because his grandmother didn't wake him up. When he awoke, she was still lying next to him. When he tried to wake her, he couldn't. She had died lying next to him sometime during the night. Even though he was overcome with grief, he built her coffin and make sure she had a nice funeral. He never slept in that bed again, and shortly afterward he moved out of that house. He was eighteen years old then.

When my father first told me this story, I threw myself at him at the end of it, and we both started to cry—he just a little, I quite a lot. It was a Sunday afternoon; he and my mother and I had gone for a walk in the botanical gardens. My mother had wandered off to look at some strange kind of thistle, and we could see her as she bent over the bushes to get a closer look and reach out to touch the leaves of the plant. When she returned to us and saw that we had both been crying, she started to get quite worked up, but my father quickly told her what had happened and she laughed at us and called us her little fools. But then she took me in her arms and kissed me, and she said that I needn't worry about such a thing as her sailing off or dying and leaving me all alone in the world. But if ever after that I saw my father sitting alone with a faraway look on his face, I was filled with pity for him. He had been alone in the world all that time, what with his mother sailing off on a boat with his father and his never seeing her again, and then his grandmother dying while lying next to him in the middle of the night. It was more than anyone should have to bear. I loved him so and wished that I had a mother to give him, for, no matter how much my own mother loved him, it could never be the same.

When my mother got through with the trunk, and I had heard again and again just what I had been like and who had said what to me at what point in my life, I was given my tea—a cup of cocoa and a buttered bun. My father by then would return home from work, and he was given his tea. As my mother went around preparing our supper, picking up clothes from the stone heap, or taking clothes off the clothesline, I would sit in a corner of our yard and watch her. She never stood still. Her powerful legs carried her from one part of the yard to the other, and in and out of the house. Sometimes she might call out to me to go and get some thyme or basil or some other herb for her, for she grew all her herbs in little pots that she kept in a corner of our little garden. Sometimes when I gave her the herbs, she might stoop down and kiss me on my lips and then on my neck. It was in such a paradise that I lived.

The summer of the year I turned twelve, I could see that I had grown taller; most of my clothes no longer fit. When I could get a dress over my head, the waist then came up to just below my chest. My legs had become more spindlelike, the hair on my head even more unruly than usual, small tufts of hair had appeared under my arms, and when I perspired the smell was strange, as if I had turned into a strange animal. I didn't say anything about it, and my mother and father didn't seem to notice, for they didn't say anything, either. Up to then, my mother and I had many dresses made out of the same cloth, though hers had a different, more grownup style, a boat neck or a sweetheart neckline, and a pleated or gored skirt, while my dresses had high necks with collars, a deep hemline, and, of course, a sash that tied in the back. One day, my mother and I had gone to get some material for new dresses to celebrate her birthday (the usual gift from my father), when I came upon a piece of cloth—a yellow background, with figures of men, dressed in a long-ago fashion, seated at pianos that they were playing, and all around them musical notes flying off into the air. I immediately said how much I loved this piece of cloth and how nice I thought it would look on us both, but my mother replied, "Oh, no. You are getting too old for that. It's time you had your own clothes. You just cannot go around the rest of your life looking like a little me." To say that I felt the earth swept away from under me would not be going too far. It wasn't just what she said, it was the way she said it. No accompanying little laugh. No bending over and kissing my little wet forehead (for suddenly I turned hot, then cold, and all my pores must have opened up, for fluids just flowed out of me). In the end, I got my dress with the men playing their pianos, and my mother got a dress with red and yellow overgrown hibiscus, but I was never able to wear my own dress or see my mother in hers without feeling bitterness and hatred, directed not so much toward my mother as toward, I suppose, life in general.

As if that were not enough, my mother informed me that I was on the verge of becoming a young lady, so there were quite a few things I would have to do differently. She didn't say exactly what it was that made me on the verge of becoming a young lady, and I was glad of that, because I didn't want to know. Behind a closed door, I stood naked in front of a mirror and looked at myself from head to toe. I was so long and bony that I more than filled up the mirror, and my small ribs pressed out against my skin. I tried to push my unruly hair down against my head so that it would lie flat, but as soon as I let it go it bounced up again. I could see the small tufts of hair under my arms. And then I got a good look at my nose. It had suddenly spread across my face, almost blotting out my cheeks, taking up my whole face, so that if I didn't know I was me standing there I would have wondered about that strange girl—and to think that only so recently my nose had been a small thing, the size of a rosebud. But what could I do? I thought of begging my mother to ask my father if he could build for me a set of clamps into which I could screw myself at night before I went to sleep and which would surely cut back on my growing. I was about to ask her this when I remembered that a few days earlier I had asked in my most pleasing, winning way for a look through the trunk. A person I did not recognize answered in a voice I did not recognize, "Absolutely not! You and I don't have time for that anymore." Again, did the ground wash out from under me? Again, the answer would have to be yes, and I wouldn't be going too far.

Because of this young-lady business, instead of days spent in perfect harmony with my mother, I trailing in her footsteps, she showering down on me her kisses and affection and attention, I was now sent off to learn one thing and another. I was sent to someone who knew all about manners and how to meet and greet important people in the world. This woman soon asked me not to come again, since I could not resist making farting-like noises each time I had to practice a curtsy, it made the other girls laugh so. I was sent for piano lessons. The piano teacher, a shriveled-up old spinster from Lancashire, England, soon asked me not to come back, since I seemed unable to resist eating from the bowl of plums she had placed on the piano purely for decoration. In the first case, I told my mother a lie—I told her that the manners teacher had found that my manners needed no improvement, so I needn't come anymore. This made her very pleased. In the second case, there was no getting around it—she had to find out. When the piano teacher told her of my misdeed, she turned and walked away from me, and I wasn't sure that if she had been asked who I was she wouldn't have said, "I don't know," right then and there. What a new thing this was for me: my mother's back turned on me in disgust. It was true that I didn't spend all my days at my mother's side before this, that I spent most of my days at school, but before this young-lady business I could sit and think of my mother, see her doing one thing or another, and always her face bore a smile for me. Now I often saw her with the corners of her mouth turned down in disapproval of me. And why was my mother carrying my new state so far? She took to pointing out that one day I would have my own house and I might want it to be a different house from the one she kept. Once, when showing me a way to store linen, she patted the folded sheets in place and said, "Of course, in your own house you might choose another way." That the day might actually come when we would live apart I had never believed. My throat hurt from the tears I held bottled up tight inside. Sometimes we would both forget the new order of things and would slip into our old ways. But that didn't last very long.

In the middle of all these new things, I had forgotten that I was to enter a new school that September. I had then a set of things to do, preparing for school. I had to go to the seamstress to be measured for new uniforms, since my body now made a mockery of the old measurements. I had to get shoes, a new school hat, and lots of new books. In my new school, I needed a different exercise book for each subject, and in addition to the usual—English, arithmetic, and so on—I now had to take Latin and French, and attend classes in a brand-new science building. I began to look forward to my new school. I hoped that everyone there would be new, that there would be no one I had ever met before. That way, I could put on a new set of airs; I could say I was something that I was not, and no one would ever know the difference.

On the Sunday before the Monday I started at my new school, my mother became cross over the way I had made my bed. In the center of my bedspread, my mother had embroidered a bowl over-flowing with flowers and two lovebirds on either side of the bowl. I had placed the bedspread on my bed in a lopsided way so that the embroidery was not in the center of my bed, the way it should have been. My mother made a fuss about it, and I could see that she was right and I regretted very much not doing that one little thing that would have pleased her. I had lately become careless, she said, and I could only silently agree with her.

I came home from church, and my mother still seemed to hold the bedspread against me, so I kept out of her way. At half past two in the afternoon, I went off to Sunday school. At Sunday school, I was given a certificate for best student in my study-of-the-Bible group. It was a surprise that I would receive the certificate on that day, though we had known about the results of a test weeks before. I rushed home with my certificate in hand, feeling that with this prize I would reconquer my mother—a chance for her to smile on me again.

When I got to our house, I rushed into the yard and called out to her, but no answer came. I then walked into the house. At first, I didn't hear anything. Then I heard sounds coming from the direction of my parents' room. My mother must be in there, I thought. When I got to the door, I could see that my mother and father were lying in their bed. It didn't interest me what they were doing—only that my mother's hand was on the small of my father's back and that it was making a circular motion. But her hand! It was white and bony, as if it had long been dead and had been left out in the elements. It seemed not to be her hand, and yet it could only be her hand, so well did I know it. It went around and around in the same circular motion, and I looked at it as if I would never see anything else in my life again. If I were to forget everything else in the world, I could not forget her hand as it looked then. I could also make out that the sounds I had heard were her kissing my father's ears and his mouth and his face. I looked at them for I don't know how long.

When I next saw my mother, I was standing at the dinner table that I had just set, having made a tremendous commotion with knives and forks as I got them out of their drawer, letting my parents know that I was home. I had set the table and was now half standing near my chair, half draped over the table, staring at nothing in particular and trying to ignore my mother's presence. Though I couldn't remember our eyes having met, I was quite sure that she had seen me in the bedroom, and I didn't know what I would say if she mentioned it. Instead, she said in a voice that was sort of cross and sort of something else, "Are you going to just stand there doing nothing all day?" The something else was new;

I had never heard it in her voice before. I couldn't say exactly what it was, but I know that it caused me to reply, "And what if I do?" and at the same time to stare at her directly in the eyes. It must have been a shock to her, the way I spoke. I had never talked back to her before. She looked at me, and then, instead of saying some squelching thing that would put me back in my place, she dropped her eyes and walked away. From the back, she looked small and funny. She carried her hands limp at her sides. I was sure I could never let those hands touch me again; I was sure I could never let her kiss me again. All that was finished.

I was amazed that I could eat my food, for all or it reminded me of things that had taken place between my mother and me. A long time ago, when I wouldn't eat my beef, complaining that it involved too much chewing, my mother would first chew up pieces of meat in her own mouth and then feed it to me. When I had hated carrots so much that even the sight of them would send me into a fit of tears, my mother would try to find all sorts of ways to make them palatable for me. All that was finished now. I didn't think that I would ever think of any of it again with fondness. I looked at my parents. My father was just the same, eating his food in the same old way, his two rows of false teeth clop-clopping like a horse being driven off to market. He was regaling us with another one of his stories about when he was a young man and played cricket on one island or the other. What he said now must have been funny, for my mother couldn't stop laughing. He didn't seem to notice that I was not entertained.

My father and I then went for our customary Sunday-afternoon walk. My mother did not come with us. I don't know what she stayed home to do. On our walk, my father tried to hold my hand, but I pulled myself away from him, doing it in such a way that he would think I felt too big for that now.

That Monday, I went to my new school. I was placed in a class with girls I had never seen before. Some of them had heard about me, though, for I was the youngest among them and was said to be very bright. I liked a girl named Albertine, and I liked a girl named Gweneth. At the end of the day Gwen and I were in love, and so we walked home arm in arm together.

When I got home, my mother greeted me with the customary kiss and inquiries. I told her about my day, going out of my way to provide pleasing details, leaving out, of course, any mention at all of Gwen and my overpowering feelings for her.

MAGGIE ANDERSON

IN MY MOTHER'S HOUSE

In the dream she is never sick and it is
always summer. She wears a polished cotton
sundress with wide shoulder straps, sits calmly
in a wooden lawn chair, green, I remember

from a photograph. I wonder if she'll know me
now, but want to keep formality awhile. I shake
her hand and introduce her to my friends,
who seem more like my parents' friends than mine,

subdued, and gathering with wine glasses
on the grass. Then I'm in the house my mother's
lived in since her death and she has changed
her clothes, put on her plaid viyella shirt.

She's sitting in her attic, among suitcases
and webs of boxes. A yellow triangle of light
skims the floor into the lap of her wool skirt.
I have had to be resourceful to get to her,

climbing up a bright blue ladder to the window
that broke down as I came through, transformed
itself from glass back into sand. My mother
holds a glass jar in her hands. She seems

preoccupied, as if it's tiring to be dead.
I ask her, *Are you weary?* and she says, *No,
are you?* Yes, I say and move into her arms
for a minute only, then she says she must

be off, something pressing, like the weight
on my heart as I wake, alive now, but her body
with me still, and warm, in the silk stockings
without shoes they dressed her in for burying.

MEG KEARNEY

HELLO, MOTHER, GOODBYE

I n August of 1992, I filled out a simple form sent to me by the New York Foundling Hospital in New York City. I printed my full name as well as I knew it, my birth date and social security number; I hesitated, checked a couple of boxes, folded the form into an envelope, and walked it to the nearest mailbox.

This was my first step in what became an eight-year search for the mother I did not know, the woman who had given birth to me in June of 1964 and, five months later, had surrendered me for adoption. Ever since I was seven or eight, I had fantasized about finding her or her finding me, though for reasons both emotional and legal, I did not actively pursue my dream until I was in my late twenties. Little did I know that, instead of preparing to say hello to my mother for the very first time, I was setting myself up to say goodbye.

It is impossible to continue with this story without first clearing up an unavoidable issue: nomenclature. When discussing adoption, terminology is vitally important and inherently complicated. This is more true and more difficult for everyone concerned when the talk turns personal—when, for instance, a thirty-seven-year-old woman needs to refer to both her birthmother and adoptive mother (and so do people who associate with her, from husband to acquaintance). In my case, what seems to work in most situations is to refer to my birthmother (which seems too impersonal) as my "mother," and to my adoptive mother as my "mom," both words having loving connotations but the latter being the most intimate.

It seems I have always known I was adopted. In my house, I was the youngest of three adopted children, all of us from separate families and all from the New York Foundling, a Catholic hospital and social service agency still in existence in Manhattan. Adoption was part of the family culture—we spoke about it as a family, within our proverbial four walls and within certain boundaries, easily and even happily. My sister, brother, and I asked carefully-worded questions, knowing instinctively as we did so that some unspoken issue of family fidelity and love was on the line—we wanted information about who we were, but did not want Mom or Dad to think this meant we wanted to be "sent back." My parents shared most of what they knew about our backgrounds, and loved to tell the stories of "the phone call" that brought each of us into their lives—an adoptee's version of a birth story.

Most people know what happened on the day they were born—where their mother was when her water broke and how she did or did not make it to the hospital in time. Many people know what their father was up to during all of the excitement as well. They know how long it took to be delivered, whether or not it was an easy birth, and details of length and weight during their first hour in the world. Adoptees, on the other hand, might know what their parents were doing (laundry, packing for a long-awaited vacation) when the social worker called to say it was their lucky day: they had a three-day or six-month-old healthy baby that could be theirs if they came on over to the office and signed on the bottom line.

I loved to hear the story about "my call"—how Mom was in the kitchen when the phone rang, not expecting any news from the Foundling, as it had been five years since they'd adopted my brother and nearly eight since they'd adopted my sister. The social-worker nun said, "We know it's been a long time since you've heard from us, and you already have two children. But you wouldn't be interested in one more, would you?" Then the whole family was in the car, headed to New York City, voting on what to name me. To this day, Mom is bothered by the fact that my brother and sister were able to see me before she did, as they were whisked off to the nursery while she and Dad signed the papers.

As a child and as an adult, I was the one of the three of us who asked the most questions about my background. I was not hoping to be rescued from my parents; I felt fiercely loyal to my family and did not wish to go live with my "real mother" or anyone else. But

I was divided, longing to know who my mother was, wanting to meet someone who looked like me, and at the same time living in fear of what, as a girl, I called "the broken place," a dark where my truth lurked like a terrible secret always about to expose itself to the world. This was the secret of the flaw I was born with, the unspeakable fact that my mother had abandoned me because I was damaged from the moment of my accidental conception—that I was a mistake, unwanted and unlovable.

That my sister and brother and I were adopted was, in essence, a secret we kept from the world. Relatives and my parents' pre-children friends were the only people who knew, and the subject was never discussed even in their company, at least in front of us kids. It seemed easy to avoid, except for occasions when we would run into acquaintances in a restaurant or at church who looked at me and blithely joked, "Where'd you get her, the milk man?" I am sure this happened to my blue-eyed siblings, though we've never spoken of it—at least I had brown eyes like Mom and Dad. But by the time I went to college I was taller than everyone in my family, including my brother and father. I noticed early on in life that whenever such a quasi-amusing exchange took place, the adults would laugh and my parents would quickly change the subject. "Margaret is adopted," was never offered as an explanation. The reason for this was never discussed, either, though in my heart I carried the awful "truth" that my parents knew; they loved me in spite of the fact that I was not their flesh and blood, despite the fact that I was damaged goods. Not speaking of being adopted thus became my modus operandi as well. That as few people knew as possible seemed vital to my emotional and social survival.

Until I began my search, limits surrounding the topic of adoption were seldom tested in our house. I don't think I even realized intellectually that they existed until I was twelve, already convinced I wanted to be "an author" and just beginning to turn from writing short stories to writing poems instead. One of my first poems was about "my first mother." I wish I still had it, and only remember that it was filled with questions about who she was and if she ever wondered about me. Because my parents had encouraged my literary efforts from their stumbling start, I was eager to read Mom this draft of a new poem I'd worked on for hours. I called her into my room and sat her down on my bed. (My sister had just left for college, leaving me a room of my own.) Then I stood before her, and read it to her as seriously—and no doubt theatrically—as I could. When I looked up from my paper, I knew I'd made a mistake. Mom's face was flat, pale, impossible to read. She stood up quickly, mumbled something that sounded vaguely like praise (or so I hoped), and rushed from the room.

I don't remember what I did then. I must have known I'd crossed a boundary; I knew I had said something—my poem had done something—that carried us to a place that felt dangerous, a place I wasn't supposed to go, a place where Mom was unreachable. I knew, too, that I wasn't going back to that place again. At least in public. I continued to write poems (about my dog, and being in love and heartsick, teenage fluff ad infinitum) but showed my poems to no one until I was in my early twenties. I did not write again about adoption until my late twenties. I shared the fact that I was adopted only with my closest, most trusted friends.

Mom was understandably threatened when she realized how often and how passionately I thought about my birthmother. Still, Mom always spoke kindly of her, and made a point of explaining that she was no ordinary woman. She did not have many details about my background, but Mom knew that my mother had written some kind of letter or list of stipulations to the nuns at the New York Foundling, an outline of what she wanted for me in terms of a life and a family that exactly described her and Dad and my sister and brother. Otherwise, I'd never have been placed where I was, in a home "already lucky enough to have two adopted children." Maybe it was this story, this knowledge, that enabled me to feel with near certainty that my mother had never forgotten me.

My "other mother" played an active and ever-changing role in my imagination for as long as I can remember. Nearly three decades is ample time for anyone, especially a fledgling poet, to develop a phantasmagorical picture of her birthmother and what finding her would be like. Some of my girlish images painted her as Audrey Hepburn in *My Fair Lady*: an impoverished but highly intelligent and spirited woman who not been treated well by life. As my version played itself out, she would, in time, rise above all obstacles, blossom into her own best self, and then come knocking at my door, full of explanations, begging forgiveness.

Other times, I pictured my mother as a famous novelist, a Jane Austen scribbling at her desk morning and night. This fierce and brilliant artist could not possibly both pen The Great Novel and raise a child. But I was no ordinary child! Ah, there was the rub— if she had kept me, my novelist-mother would have realized that I would be her perfect, quiet girl—always reading in a corner, never disturbing her work, occasionally bringing her coffee and buttered toast. But—there were always too many "buts" in these stories— my mother didn't know that.

One version of this story ended, sadly, there. In a more hopeful revision, she would (once her career was unquestionably launched) write me a long letter explaining why she'd given me up and asking if I would possibly consider coming to New York (where such a famous author undoubtedly lived) to meet her. I wouldn't simply run to her, either. We would exchange a series of letters, a debate of sorts in which I—wowing her with my own literary prowess—would make her see how wrong she'd been to let me go. Sometimes I would not reply to her letters at all, but she (nearly frantic by then, realizing her mistake) would write again and again. She would have to grovel before I finally agreed to come visit her at her Park Avenue flat.

And then I'd be there, at her door—she'd open it, and gasp. We looked exactly alike! We even wore the same color shirt (orange or purple or black, depending on what year it was in my life). We'd hug and kiss and cry for hours. We'd sing along with Carole King records and recite Robert Frost and drink hot chocolate. I'd fast become her muse, her confidante, her first reader, her trusted soul-mate. She would write a best-selling novel about me. I'd write a best-selling book of poems about us.

These are the stories that saved me, that snatched me by the scruff of my neck and yanked me from "the broken place," a well dug far beyond the point of self-pity to the depths of a sadness, a sense of loss so fathomless I knew it had the power to suffocate me.

Once I became an adult, the essence of the images I had conjured of my mother changed very little. She was never a prostitute or homeless, though sometimes she was in desperate straits, living hand-to-mouth in a crumbling, five-story walk-up in the South Bronx; sometimes she was promiscuous, sometimes just a gullible girl who lacked the self-assurance to say no to the men who lavished her with compliments. She was always smart, always spent countless hours in either bookstores (which she'd never leave empty-handed) or at the library, the poor-woman's college.

Still, I was haunted as much by what I did not know as what I was told. "Your mother loved you so much, she gave you up so you could have a better life." This was the most confusing and most-often quoted line I remember from my childhood. It was said with the best intentions, meant to soothe my pain and satisfy my curiosity, though it was taboo to talk about either pain or curiosity in any depth, and the idea of it only aggravated both. *"Better?"* Than what? How can my life be better than a life I didn't have a chance to live? Was my mother insane, or in prison? Was giving me away really for my benefit, or for hers? What kind of love is it that leads to such a separation? What kind of world is it that forces a woman to feel she must give up her daughter? These are questions that I continue to struggle with, in a more empathetic and mature way now than I did as a child. I have met many adoptees over the last ten years who tell me their adoptive parents said the same thing to them. I'm convinced it was a line that originated in either a "Now That You've Adopted a Child" pamphlet or in a similarly titled self-help book.

Despite or because of my endless, private questioning and myriad fantasies, the sense that my mother had not forgotten me remained strong right up through my adulthood and eventual search for her. This instinct was especially profound on my birthday; and perhaps it was what allowed me the emotional freedom to create a rather cinematic series of reunion scenarios in my mind. Most of these were happy scenes, which ran the gamut of her finding me (she nervously dialing my number from the payphone on the corner—though there was no such thing on the suburban street where I grew up—to ask permission to see me) to our meeting by chance (she and I unwittingly laying our blankets side-by-side at the beach, or on the lawn at a Joni Mitchell concert, and staring at each other in instant recognition and joyful disbelief. Frantic hugging and crying then ensued).

These mini-made-for-Meg movies began to widen in scope after I began my formal search for my mother in 1992. Suddenly, I was forced to consider possibilities other than the happy reunions. It was time to be honest with myself. My mother might not want to be found. She might not be receptive, might not even be willing to speak on the phone, if I did find her. Ah, yes—there was that: if I did find her. I made myself face the fact that I might not ever know her or meet her in person. But I never imagined—never allowed myself to consider what, in the end, was the truth.

At the beginning of my search—that day in the summer of 1992 when I filled out that form—I had convinced myself that I was seeking medical information only. This way, I didn't have to face issues of loyalty or misunderstandings by my adoptive family, namely my mom and older brother and sister, with whom I am still extremely close. I had already come to the necessary realization that searching for my mother had nothing to do with how much I loved and appreciated my parents and siblings, but wasn't yet sure I could convince them of that. My dad had died in 1990. I felt that he was watching over me, nodding his approval and blessing.

The form I sent to the Foundling had invited me to check the appropriate boxes to indicate what kind of information I wanted. At first I simply checked "medical history" but was fascinated by another, something to the effect of "hobbies and interests." Just before I sealed the envelope, I checked that box as well, and mailed it before I could change my mind.

Looking back, I realize I had not prepared myself for what I had just asked for, or for what I was about to learn. The three-page letter that arrived in September, 1992, read like a novel. To learn something as basic as one's true ethnicity—I grew up being told I was half Irish, half German/Austrian, only to learn I am more Scottish than Irish, and perhaps half French—is stunning, to say the least. But to learn, at age 28, the circumstances of my birth and relinquishment — that story sent me into a tailspin that made me dizzy for months. It was two years before I felt ready to take another step.

In adoption-agency terms, what I had received from the Foundling was "non-identifying information"—what facts they could provide about the circumstances of my birth without revealing who my mother was. The letter disclosed that when I was born, my mother was 25 years old and a devout Catholic. She was college-educated and working as a teacher on Long Island. In her words, she'd gone through "a wild period" in her early 20s, during which time she met my birthfather. They dated for four months, but had already broken things off when she realized she was pregnant. She decided "not to involve him." This was not surprising; it was 1964. She was unmarried, pregnant, and living in her home town, where aunts and uncles and cousins abounded, and everybody knew everybody. The scandal had the potential to ruin her life and reputation—not to mention the stain on the family name.

The letter also said that my mother had entered the New York Foundling's unwed mother unit in February of 1964. (Her mother— my grandmother—told family and friends that my mother was in Arizona looking for a job, as she was interested in moving out west. The only thing true about this story, I learned much later, was that my mother was indeed interested in moving west.) The letter also revealed that at first my mother "spoke mechanically about adoption," and spent many hours in the chapel crying, "trying to make a prayerful decision." After I was born in June, my mother had still not signed anything, and I was placed in foster care. I had some minor medical problems that would have delayed my placement anyway, and so she had more time to think. Whenever I was scheduled for a doctor's appointment, she and her mother would meet me at the doctor's office.

My mother signed my surrender papers on October 28. She was given a photograph of me to keep. She is quoted as saying, "I have never experienced such heartfelt torment." On November 14, I was placed in my adoptive home.

So this was the mother I was looking for—one for whom giving me up had not been easy, a person who might welcome me if I knocked on her door, who might, in some way, be the woman of my fantasies. This new insight, though it didn't guarantee anything, gave me strength throughout most of the years of my search, when I had a scattered and sometimes shaky support system. The men in my life came and went every three years or so. My closest girlfriend, who grew up across the street from me and knew me better than anyone besides my sister, by then lived on another coast, and for a while in another country. I didn't feel that I could tell Mom, or my sister and brother, until I'd already been looking for several years; and when I finally did, they all gave me their blessing, though they were obviously worried about both my getting hurt and their somehow "losing" me to my blood relatives. I couldn't discuss my worst fears with them, as they were already conjuring up enough of their own.

After moving to Manhattan from upstate New York in 1994, I did discover an adoptee search-and-support group, which met regularly on the Upper East Side. For the first time, I was able to talk with other adoptees—and two birthmothers—and know that they understood firsthand what it was like to be me. The group's founder and leader, also an adoptee, helped me sort through my multi-faceted, complicated fears surrounding my search, the highest on the list being that of rejection—another form of abandonment.

The support group provided a steady source of sympathetic listeners and information about the endlessly frustrating process of searching, but my fellow members could not be there for me 24/7. I needed another source of strength, another outlet, at three a.m. when I was lying awake trying to picture what my mother looked like, or what her life had been before and after I was born, or—by the time I'd discovered my last name in 1998—scheming about how I was going to find a 60-year-old woman named Smith.

That outlet, I realized, was poetry. The few poems I'd written about being adopted or about my mother were, number one, terrible; and, number two, barely scratched the surface of what I was really feeling (which is, in part, what made them so terrible). It wasn't until the mid-90s that I began exploring this subject honestly and recurrently in my work. What surprised me most about these poems, why I felt good and at the same terrified by them, was that—in my mind—they had "outed" me. To my own astonishment, I thought I had officially "come out of the closet" as an adoptee, an idea that filled me with dread and terror because anyone who read the poems would know the essential and awful truth about me, the secret flaw I'd kept hidden all that time. But even as I feared "everyone is going to know," few did. The poems could be understood on more than one level, none of which necessarily had to do with adoption. Two poet friends of mine actually read several of these poems and each said he wondered if I'd ever start to write more explicitly. Well, I have opened up about the subject of adoption, both in my writing and in my relationships with people. (Yet this essay, I admit, feels way over the line for me, at moments shooting erratic pangs of terror through my chest.)

It was in 1998, when I was deeply involved in writing these poems, that the leader of the support group put me in touch with a private investigation agency that (illegally) profits by reuniting adoptees with their birthparent or parents. When I tell this story, many people are surprised, even outraged, to learn that what I did was against the law. It most states, including New York, adoption records remain closed. Just as I have no legal right to know anything more about my origins than what is contained in the non-identifying information provided me by the New York Foundling, I have no legal right to my original birth certificate, locked in a file somewhere in Albany. The certificate in my possession is dated two years after I was born, when the adoption was finalized, under the name given me by my adoptive parents: Margaret Mary Kearney.

The search for my mother entered its final phase soon after I contacted the private investigator who, given what information I could provide, said she could find my mother. That October, I sold my pickup truck and signed the contract. Now I had the cash, and was told the process would take between three weeks and six months. No money would change hands until my mother had been located. I began to wait.

Thus began one of most world-tipping years of my life. On December 26, 1998, I flew from New York to Lynchburg, Virginia, and shared a cab with a handsome redhead to the Virginia Center for the Creative Arts, an artists' colony where I planned to spend two weeks writing and reading, being a hermit. Little did I know that I was about to fall in love with the man who paid half the cab fare.

Mike and I were engaged seven weeks later, when I flew out to California to see him for Valentine's Day. Then he came home to New York with me, to meet my family and help deliver our big news. It was during his visit that my other big news arrived. The investigator called. She'd found my mother. All I had to do was wire her the money, and she would e-mail me all of the information.

On Thursday, February 25, 1999, I made a plan with Mike. "The e-mail" was due to arrive by 3:00 P.M., and I had to go to work. He would go to The New York Public Library, a few minutes' walk from my office building, and then call me just after three, ready for whatever.

Throughout the day, it was nearly impossible for me to concentrate. I spent the last hour pacing my office. Before I knew it, I would have my mother's name and phone number. I would have her address. I'd already told myself that I would write her a letter instead of calling, though by 2:45, I wasn't sure if I would be able to resist dialing her number—at least calling her answering machine, if she wasn't home, to hear her voice. Then maybe I'd hang up. The office suddenly felt like the inside of a refrigerator. I was shaking. At three o'clock I stared at my computer, then picked up the phone and called the investigator. Had she sent the e-mail? I was too terrified to check without knowing first. Yes, she told me, the message would be in my in-box. "But I'm glad you called," she said, "because it's better I tell this to you over the phone. Then you can print out my e-mail, and go home, and call me from there."

"Why? What's wrong?" I shivered uncontrollably.

She said, "Your mother is dead. I'm sorry."

I felt part of me separate at this news, the part that has the power to hover and watch my life unfolding as if it were a movie. The part that removes itself at moments when I might otherwise fall into that well and never find myself again. Mike called; I asked him to meet me in front of my building as soon as he could. I opened my e-mail, and while the note printed I put on my coat. The staff asked no questions when I said I wasn't feeling well, that I was going home.

Mike was within sight by the time I reached the street. I hailed a cab, which pulled up just as Mike reached me. We hugged and got in. The look on my face must have been clue enough for him not to ask me any questions. My only words were directions to the taxi driver. I knew I could not speak, could not repeat what the investigator had told me, until I was home, until I had closed the door to my apartment and it was safe for me to say it—to let the words out like a rabid animal, dangerous and unpredictable: my mother is dead.

It was pure grace that brought Mike into my life just in time to catch me at that moment. I am not sure how I would have managed if I had been alone. But he was my comfort and my anchor in those first hours of raving and grief, and my source of calm. Because of him, I was able to read the e-mail message, to learn my mother's name, to learn that she had died of breast cancer in 1983. Strange to the point of being spooky, it happened that the day before, the day I had wired the money, was the anniversary of her death: February 24.

As if that weren't enough, my name at birth—the name my mother gave me—was the same name given me by my adoptive parents: Margaret Mary. When I brought this up with Mom weeks later, it revived a memory she had of completing the documents necessary to take me home with a nun at the Foundling who— upon hearing what Mom and Dad had decided to name me— immediately dropped her pen and went running down the hallway "to tell everyone." It turns out that most of the first-born girls in the Smith clan are named Margaret, and the nuns knew how important it would have been to my mother to know that I would keep my name, if only they were allowed to tell her.

The revelations contained in the investigator's e-mail did not stop there. I discovered that I had an aunt and uncle who were alive—the aunt within driving distance. But even more amazing, I had another brother and sister, both alive, too, and living on the West Coast. I would never meet my mother—it might take a lifetime to come to terms with that—but I had hope again: of pictures, of stories of her, of meeting people who looked like me, of knowing people related to me by blood.

I now have in my possession a photocopy of a letter my mother wrote to the Foundling in August of 1964, the "famous" letter in which she outlined her hopes for me: a Catholic upbringing outside of the City, siblings, and loving parents who were involved in either the medical or educational fields (Mom was an RN, Dad a school principal)—in essence, she had described my family, the Kearney's.

But perhaps my mother's most remarkable wish for me was intangible. Her own words say it best: "a home where education, formal education and self-education through reading, etc., plays a central role in the everyday. So many doors are open to the mind that is filled with the beauties to be found everywhere—in nature, poetry, music. The person who is out to learn all that is good sees so much more in everyday life and lives a much richer existence than the one who remains passive in the doldrums of routine... Dear God, how I'd love to guide her myself! Knowing she is in a home similar to what I would want to give her will be of much consolation." So—she was a writer, after all.

Today, I have two families who embrace me and each other. I grew up the youngest of three, and now I am also the oldest of three, with a brother and sister on either side. Now I cannot imagine my life without my "little" brother and sister, my "new" uncle and aunt. And with their help, I have begun to know my mother, Elizabeth. I've heard her voice on tape; I know she kept a journal, enjoyed a glass of wine at the end of the day, loved to dance, and could cook a mean burrito. I know that, like me, she wore silver and turquoise jewelry. My uncle says we have the same laugh. Perhaps best of all, by my relatives' dumbfounded stares and knowing smiles, I believe that what I want to see in photographs is true: I, more than anyone else, look like my mother.

The first time I visited my aunt in upstate New York, she took me to my mother's grave. Elizabeth had lived and died in Arizona, but her husband and my brother and sister flew with her ashes back to New York so she could be buried near her parents. When the car pulled into the cemetery, I felt myself separating again— watching myself open the door, step out, and approach the headstone. I often return to this scene in my life, shouting in my head as if at a movie I can't help but watch again and again, fast-forwarding or rewinding to this moment where the script has taken a profoundly upsetting turn: *It wasn't supposed to go like this, mother. This isn't how I pictured it.* This is it, all I can think, the closest I come to prayer. And then I remove one of my earrings, a favorite silver and turquoise piece shaped like a wing, which I have owned for years. I dig a little hole and bury it. And then I say goodbye.

PAMELA SCHOENEWALDT

Tell Her, Then Go

"My hair stands on end when I'm talking to my mom," my adopted daughter Anna tells her therapist. "Sometimes just her face makes me angry." It's true. Anna stiffens when I walk in the room, more and more since her breasts began to bloom. Now that she's crossed menarche, her beautiful eyes launch dark spears at me.

For the past month, my house has been occupied, nearly possessed by Tanya, a short, wide Bulgarian woman, Anna's birth mother. I rarely see this Tanya, but I feel her loom behind me whenever I fight with Anna. Tanya is shorter than I am, but I know she looms. Thick gray smoke pours from her Balkan cigarettes, clouds the air around me and makes it stink. When I speak to Anna of homework, curfews, or not leaving wet towels on the floor, Tanya makes ugly faces behind my back and Anna screams, "Bitch, I hate you." If I push the point—any point, it seems these days—Anna's bound to close with: "If you don't like me how I am, send me to an institute, I don't care. You aren't my real mom anyway." Then she stomps away. When her door slams shut, the whole house shakes.

Anna was "an older child adoption," so a Bulgarian judge asked her: "Do you want to emigrate? Do you want this new family? Do you understand what adoption means?" Anna answered, "Yes, oh yes." But that was then. Now she screams: "I was wrong. I didn't know what a shitty mom you'd be."

"It's too late now," I shout back when I'm angry. "I'm the best you've got."

Of course we do have lighter moments. When we shop, sometimes when we cook, she giggles and plays. When she's sick she lets me hold or even read to her, old as she is, saying, "Nobody did this for me before." And sometimes when Anna's chewing gum she takes a pink, sugar-reeking wad from her mouth and waves it

110

at Tanya, right in my face. "See?" Anna gloats, "I have real gum now." She crams it her mouth, spraying drops of spit. In Bulgaria she chewed soft asphalt in the summer when her mother housed her by a newly paved road. She didn't know better and nobody told her not to.

But she knew other things. She knew when to leave. Tanya brought home men, or moved in with them. If she couldn't store her kids someplace, she brought them too. Cramped, drunk, tired of noise, one of these men threw Anna's baby sister out the window. It was snowing. Anna and her mother scavenged in the dark, feeling the frozen ground through shards of glass until they found the cold, bruised baby, too stunned to cry. Anna was five years old. "Wait until he's sleeping," she whispered to Tanya, "and then we'll run away." They did just that, packing quietly, muffling the baby, and hurrying through unlit streets to a new man's house, perhaps her birth father's.

"Good," I say carefully to this story, "you knew how to take care of yourself." I don't mention what I know: this man, if he was her birth father, ran from her birth certificate, leaving no trace of his name behind.

It's November. Anna's grades are in freefall. "I don't care about school," she says, "I'll be poor anyway when I grow up." Once my husband could help her study. No more. And he's often gone, like now. He just called to say he's sorry, but a project due to end this Friday will last through Wednesday night. Tanya stays in corners when my husband's home. Now she'll be at my back all weekend.

"Oh yeah," Anna mocks when I explain her father's change of plans. "I bet 'Something came up.' I'll bet you even believe that." In fact I do believe, but why should Anna, I ask myself over and over, when for years every man around either hurt or left her?

Saturday morning, very late, I try to rouse her, "Anna, it's your turn to rake the leaves."

She turns over in bed, her untouched school books slung on the floor. "Later," she mumbles. "Get a life." Afternoon, a brown curled carpet still coats the lawn. Anna's watching television. "I did it, the

111

wind blew down more," she insists, pointing the TV control at me, pressing "Mute." There was no wind today, I point out. Soon she's screaming: "It's the truth! Why can't you believe me?"

Now I do feel wind at my neck, my hair on end. Tanya's behind me, blowing acrid smoke and angry words. I can guess what she's saying, even in a language I don't know: "Don't listen to this thin woman, Americanski. She's nobody to you, just documents. It's blood between you and me. I'm your real mother, I knit your bones, I made your heart. Don't do shit for her. One day she'll take you to an institute and leave you there. Count on it. I know what you do to mothers. You make us crazy, you lazy, stupid, worthless girl. Aren't you grateful you're in America now? Why don't you rake like the nice lady wants?"

When Tanya turns away, we're stinking in her smoke, dazed and fighting over leaves again. I breathe deeply and try to remember, as my husband says, just who's the child here.

I'll rake the lawn myself, I'm about to conclude; it's pointless to push this one. But now Anna knocks over a flower vase, screaming, "I won't touch your goddamn lawn, not now, not ever. Get it? Get it!" And she's gone. In the ringing silence all I can manage is the dull obvious. I write "no" on a chore calendar hung on the kitchen wall. For weeks, a row of "no." So no allowance this week. "And I won't get my allowance, you don't have to tell me," Anna screams from the next room.

"Demonstrate cause and effect," our therapist insists, "give consistent rewards and consequences. Eventually it sinks in." While I demonstrate cause and effect, I feel Tanya's breath behind me, close as a shadow. She must know I'm claustrophobic. She smells like she's worn the same clothes for years, tobacco laced with sweat, soaked into synthetics.

I turn quickly and she steps back, pudgy face smirking at me. This is the first time I've seen her face. Where did her daughter's delicate lines come from, high cheekbones, that lift to the chin, the fine turn of the jaw? Tanya face is puffed, perhaps from rakia— vodka-clear, 100 proof wine. She seems to have an endless supply

112

of Bulgarian booze and tobacco. And that smirk—I see it daily on a smaller face.

Tanya's bracelets jangle like dull bells. She digs another pack of smokes from inside her shirt. Is she padded with packs? Is that why she's fat? Much more than this is running me, of course, layers more to dig through with my therapist, but right now, I'm choking: "Stop that! Don't smoke in my house!" I doubt she understands English, although I point to her hand and wave at the smoke rolling over me. She laughs a high yelp and mimics: "Don't schmoke in my house!" Her ashes disappear on the bright kitchen floor.

When I grab for her smoking hand, she skitters away to the dining room. What would I do if I got her? Shake her like a rag? What good is that? I try to step back, pump up reason to rule me, put myself in this woman's shoes: ignorant and poor, no skills to sell and losing her looks in a disintegrating post-Soviet Second World, no social services, no private therapists to help, hunting men who'll trade for room and board, rakia and smokes, her ragged children screaming, thrown from windows, chewing asphalt, her lovely little daughter too much noticed by boyfriends, uncles, and old men. All this may be true and yet of these two mothers, one signed papers: I relinquish, I renounce, I give up this child forever. The other signed: yes, forever. So whose house is this and whose daughter now? "Go away!" I point to the door. This much the woman has to understand: pointing, doors. "Nyet," she shouts back, stamping her feet and planting herself like a stake in my house.

Our shouting brings Anna, gripping the station changer. Will she mute us both? When Tanya turns to stare at her, Anna's hard, lovely face thaws and cracks, like winter passing, all her teenage sureness melted down to bewilderment and rage. Now she cries at Tanya what must be: "Why did you give me away? Why me? What did I do? Tell me!"

I know the meaning of a shrug. Perhaps Tanya just can't say, "I had pain myself. I did what I had to. I did what was best for you.

I did what he told me to do." Yet here is Anna facing her, ravenous for words. And here am I between them. Tanya fiddles with her necklace and flicks ashes from her skirt.

All the business with the leaves, all our other business shrinks to smaller than a necklace bead. "Tell her! Give the kid some peace!" I shout. Tanya turns to gaze at me as if I were a pointlessly barking dog. "Explain!" I shout again. "I want some peace myself. Tell her, then go! Leave, get out of this house!"

Tanya does turn away from us, but not to leave. There is a table near our front door, waist high in the crook of the stairway. We use it for mail, for keys and objects on their way upstairs. Tanya pushes everything aside and climbs up on the table. Her wide self and skirt fill the space.

"Tell her she can't stay," I tell Anna. "It was bad enough when I couldn't see her. Tell her I don't want her in this house, I want her out of here." Anna translates.

Tanya rests her head against the banister and lights another cigarette. "I don't care," she must be saying. "What will you do now, Lady, call the Police?"

"Tell her I won't feed her, ever," I try.

Now Anna stiffens. "Don't be so stingy, Mom."

"I don't care. I'm very stingy. This is the House of Stingy, tell her that."

Smoke is thicker now, a cloud. I can barely see Tanya inside it. Keys fly, knocking, scraping, is she ripping my house down?

"Stop that!" I shout.

The smoke clears. Suddenly I know what Tanya's saying: "I would have kept you if I had a house like this."

Evidently Anna doesn't buy this. Now they're screaming in Bulgarian. Strange to hear my daughter wild in a language I don't know. But I read from her face what she's doing—throwing back loneliness, anger, asphalt gum, promises and lies, babies lying stunned in shards of glass, cots in other people's houses grudgingly made up, cousins pushed over to make room, men (uncles? grandfathers? mother's boyfriends?) wanting her in their own

114

cots, cots in orphanages—no breakfast if the sheets aren't straight, Amerikanski coming, English, big changes, homework, all the jangling pulls and choices in America. Anna screaming, Tanya staring back, smoking.

Anna is exhausted; her slight shoulders shake. I grab her and say, "Stop now, shh. We'll just ignore her, maybe she'll leave."

Anna sighs, pure Balkan teenager: moms and Americans, don't they get how dumb they are? In fact, what do I know of life on the other side? Do I really think that if you study hard, pay your bills, and clean your house, then things work out? What do I know of life in an occupied land? The Ottomans held Bulgaria five hundred years, the Soviets almost fifty. But here in this house we can't wait much longer for this occupation to end. Already Anna's little life is fraying: steady failures every day at school, distrust, anger and weariness with a life crammed so full of pain so early. "Life's going to be hard for her," the therapist warned us, "hard for a very long time. I can't promise you she'll make it."

"No, Mom, she won't go away," Anna says in tones she uses for "No, Mom, I shouldn't be studying."

"Well then," I suggest, "suppose she stays here, but leaves us alone in the other rooms. What do you think?"

Anna cocks her head to consider me. Is it so rare that I ask for her opinion? Perhaps it is. She's breathing hard. "I'll tell her she can't move from there," Anna hazards. "We could keep the keys on the coffee table." I could have guessed—Anna hates when I clean off the table; now there's excuse for clutter. ("It's everybody's table. How come you're so picky?")

I look at the cherry-dark wood of the table, a smooth oval lake, calming to see. "I guess we could do that," I agree. When we move keys and mail, Tanya glares at us.

All that weekend, each time Anna stomps past the table on the way up to her room, she barks into the smoky cloud: "Why? Tell me why!" From the cloud comes, "No," or "I don't know." Never more than this. Sometimes, with good timing, I walk upstairs when Anna does and then the cloud is quiet. Sunday afternoon, when I've gone for groceries, Anna rakes the lawn a little. By Wednesday, Tanya has drifted from the landing, although the acrid smell remains.

COLETTE INEZ

RIVER HOUSE INVENTIONS

Blistered hands raw on the oars,
I row past her house, call out her name
or

sailing past the river house,
I wave to the woman on the dock.
She crochets memories
she will throw over her lap.

Anchored to childhood, moored
to old age, she rocks in her chair,
watches the river
turn into a cloud the shape of a girl reading a book.

But I can annihilate the boat, make the river
disappear, plant the house on a plateau or a hill.
I can have the woman on the dock look out
through French windows at the river and sky,
make her believe in the power of prayer.

I can re-invent my parentage. Not father-priest,
but father-baker, hair the color of daily bread.
Not mother-archivist, but mother-sailor-with-a-crew
steering a course for the Argentine.

In a limousine I may carry a cone of roses,
and a book of common prayer, want to say
"I am your daughter,"
but do not when she floats to the door.
Spectral woman, she beckons me into her house,
unties the cord, cuts the roses on a slant,
slips them in a milkglass vase.

She looks at me when I look elsewhere.
I look at her, her milk white hair.
In the vestibule mirror
she is what I might be and am not.

But if I push the boat back into the river, pull
on the oars, fashion myself into a girl struggling to sail,
calling out to be seen, then what?
What has gone on between the woman and her child?

"Curious," she might say to a visitor, a priest
come to share church talk and a cup of tea. "I saw a girl
wave to me from a boat. She called out my name.
It was no one I knew." How very odd, they will agree.

This is true. A proper daughter in a proper suit, I knock
at her door for the second time in thirty years.
We nod, pump hands, say where we've been.
I don't know who she is and will not know even after
death strolls up from the river to take her in his arms.

And she will not know I have become
a visible woman, full of inventions.

MARILYN CHIN

Take a Left at the Waters of Samsara

There is a bog of sacred water
    Behind a hedgerow of wild madder
Near the grave of my good mother
    Tin cans blossom there

The rust shimmers like amber
    A diorama of green gnats
Ecstatic in their veil dance
    A nation of frogs regale

Swell-throated, bass-toned
    One belts and rages, the others follow
They fuck blissfully
    Trapped in their cycle

Of rebirth, transient love
    Unprepared for higher ground
And I, my mother's aging girl
    Myopic, goat-footed

Got snagged on an unmarked trail
    The road diverged; I took
The one less traveled
    Blah, blah

I sit at her grave for hours
    A slow drizzle purifies my flesh
I still yearn for her womb
    And can't detach

I chant new poems, my best fascicle
    Stupid pupil, the truth
Is an oxymoron and exact
    Eternity can't be proven to the dead

What is the void but motherlessness?
    The song bellies up
The sun taketh
    The rain ceases to bless

MOIRA CRONE

WITH AN EYEBROW PENCIL

O ther summers she'd worked on an archeological dig; gone to Israel on a fellowship; studied grass-roots organizing; aced a course in college logic; interned at a rock magazine. In the fall, she was off for Yale. But that June before she left, our daughter Anya took her place behind a counter in a tiny stucco storefront five blocks from our old house in New Orleans and started selling bagels. At six, she closed up, rushed back to change, and went out to join her friends who were milling around that summer like planes on a hot night runway, engines idling, waiting for the signal to queue up and take off.

I was supposed to go to Prague with my husband where he was teaching for a few weeks. Our younger child was going to a camp in Mississippi. Anya was going exactly nowhere. I think now she was waiting for me.

The day she had graduated high school, she cut her hair very short. She had been on the track team the fall and spring. She was quite strong—tall, blonde, with a long neck and wide set eyes, strong chin and brow, ears that turned out slightly. She looked like a pale blue-eyed doe.

She doesn't resemble me. She has something of my mother in her: my mother, whose beauty queen looks in the thirties and forties detracted from her other qualities—intelligence, a gift for teaching. Her own mother decided in 1925 that she would be a movie star. This seemed completely possible in Brooklyn then: after all, their next door neighbor Edith, a good looking girl who danced, became the siren Susan Hayward. My mother was no star performer, just pretty—a fact that has shaped her life, making her insecure about her abilities while she has believed religiously in the power of physical beauty.

In early June, we took a few days at the beach. I started painting

121

watercolors of all the other cottages on our strand. I had considered a career in art in college, but writing won out. I had only done a few sketches since, as a way to take a break, before I returned to my stories. This time, I couldn't stop.

When we got back from the shore, I told Rodger I couldn't go to Prague. A little stunned, he said okay. At the airport, when I hugged him goodbye, he wasn't sure what was going on. Neither was I. I had unfinished business, I announced: I had to learn to paint in oils. I had signed up for a class.

Like many lucky girls in their early teens, Anya adored her father, and her father doted on her. When she was in seventh and eighth grades, they started having conversations that left me out: her mind, very quick and discursive, was much like her father's and only a little like mine. Her attitude toward personal discipline—strict vegetarianism, marathon running—contrasted with my lapsed-Southern-Belle ways. For a while, when things were getting rocky between us, Anya and I had a policy of going to yoga together, which I felt was a respite. But one November morning, while she was shouting at me from the sidewalk that we were late, I rushed out, and slipped on the tile steps. By nightfall, my ankle had swollen to twice its size. I am terrible at rushing. That was the end of yoga for months, and of our sharing it, forever. Mom was sedentary, slow, more out of shape in every way, than Anya would have liked: she wouldn't let me forget this. I didn't concern myself that much with issues of beauty, of grooming, health, of housekeeping. I lacked discipline. Guilty as charged, I stepped back. I was hurt. At the same time I was happy to see that her father believed in her, that she knew he cared. Having lacked this myself as a girl, I was sure it was key to a woman's sense of self-worth. I kept out of the picture; I didn't make demands.

A friend of mine, the novelist Valerie Martin, said to me later, of daughters: They turn their backs on you for a time. They have to. But perhaps Anya had been turned away too long.

It wasn't as if I didn't have enough to do that summer: I had started editing for a press, I had my stories to work on—during the school year, I taught. But plein air painting took over. We met Tuesdays in Audubon Park, about seven blocks from our house. The teacher was a bit of a slave driver. I was messy, in my big splattered smock. *Discipline*, he said: *scrape your palate, keep your brushes clean.* The temperature climbed into the high nineties.

I suppose a psychiatrist could have figured out why I took this up. I wrote Rodger: "I'm growing a whole new mind." The remark of a fellow amateur, a retired Classics professor in a straw boater, might have tipped me off: "I have to visit this place everyday, it's like my mother," he said of the park.

Meanwhile, Anya and I, alone in the house, weren't talking that much. Every night she went out with her friends (some of whom had interesting jobs, my husband noted) to the clubs and cafés and parties that can make a New Orleans adolescence very alive, incredibly musical, sophisticated, a little risky.

After the first few days, she started slipping a certain topic into our morning chat. One of her high school sweethearts, after months of estrangement, was starting to call again. They had to discuss some aspect of their ended relationship, he'd announce. At ten-thirty, in some café in the Faubourg. Occasionally we went out to eat Lebanese, the best vegetarian choice. She might open up a little more with news from her friends. So and so had decided to pump espresso for the rest of this year; a certain couple, after four years of going steady, were finally breaking up. Sometime in the second week, she told me things that had happened while she was going with a boy who had hurt her, things that upset me, but it was too late: the story was over. At the time, she didn't feel she could tell me. It almost seemed as if she were sticking around that summer to get me caught up. But as soon as we started talking, someone would call, ask her out. I hardly slept until she came in. If I did doze off, I'd wake, look at the clock, and then go down the hall to make sure she was in bed. She was getting older, she could handle things, but I was getting worse that summer: I'd sneak in, and sit by her pillow listening for her breathing, the way I had when she was in the crib.

If this were a short story, the two parallel lives, daughter and mother, would converge in some dramatic incident. I might have collapsed in the incredible heat and been dragged to the bagel shop, she might have discovered a desire to come into the park with me and paint. But the truth is, we were both loners that season. But we were also developing a language, a vocabulary of examples, a way to talk about emotional things. I hardly noticed this while it was happening: I was always going out to get some more cadmium yellow.

Her father came home. Her sister came back from camp. I had an announcement. Anya was due at college the beginning of September, but in August she and I were going to New York to "buy clothes for college." My creaky Southern-Belle excuse for this extravagance—nobody could buy the right clothes for a New England fall and winter in New Orleans. Anya and I chose to ignore the fact that catalogs exist.

Looking forward to New York together was for me a way to avoid the inevitable. I suppose it was a sign of desperation on my part: I resorted to shopping as a way to bond. It sort of worked: my thrift and Anya's natural discipline combined when we got there. We'd set off in the morning into lower Manhattan with a mission— Fair Isle sweaters, snow boots, the right purse, and sometimes we came back with the goods, and sometimes we didn't. It was a form of urban hunting: exhausting, and sort of fun. I really didn't care, I'd do anything with her: she hadn't left me yet. We were talking now. We touched on destiny, how you put your life together as a woman, what's important, what's not. The difference between wanting something because other people think it is desirable and wanting something because it works for ourselves. But then she'd go out. From her travels, she had her New York cohorts who took her on the town while I sat in the hotel room, worrying, waiting.

We were staying in Chelsea. One morning, I left her, took a walk, and found an art store. I purchased what I'd not brought with me—Bristol board, oil pastels, then, at the corner market, a bouquet of sunflowers.

Anya was still asleep when I came back. I started to draw her, and draw her, sheet after sheet—her pretty face near the sunflowers, her form under the sheets. I never got it. Kept tossing them out. Sleeping beauty, something wasn't right.

Then, an editor friend suggested the Circle Line tour for two New Orleanians who had finally tired of shopping. The boat took off at a landing near the base of Manhattan. There were stalls and booths—craftspeople, small importers. I stopped to buy her some pale blue glass earrings, like little drops, to match her eyes. When I turned around she was gone. I was desolate. I felt as if, all summer, I'd been looking for her, waiting for her, trying to get her to come back, trying to capture her, hold her, keep her still. She was forever going away; I was forever praying to see her again.

First I caught sight of her back, slender and very tall in a long-sleeved white cotton shirt—and then I saw her face. There is nothing more romantic than the way a daughter's face looks to a mother. Lovers imagine they get to keep their beloved, but a mother's love is more romantic because mothers know from the day they give them birth, they will have to give them up. While some part of me was still holding out hope; another part was reconciled.

On the boat, as we were passing Ellis Island, I sketched her face with blue crayon. I got it right. She was looking around, being cool. She was wearing sunglasses, with the Statue of Liberty reflected in the lenses. Scarf on her head, something Grace Kelly-ish about the whole effect. The caption: "Anya, Launched. August 16th, 1998." I would take it home. I would put it up. In the picture she was smiling. In the picture, she was wide awake, taking off. When I drew it, I was at peace with what it meant.

They have to turn their backs on you, but then, it's okay and they turn back around, Valerie said to me.

As a child—somewhere in my mind I knew this, but had forgotten it—I used to get very sick. High fevers. Once, when I was recovering from an infection, someone set me out in my mother's beautiful garden. I had paper, colored pencils and water paints. I started doing portraits of all the flowers—pansies, daffodils, azaleas, but mostly the pansies—those indigo dark petals. My mother was

125

delighted. Interior decoration had become her obsession in middle age, as it does for so many beautiful women. She had my pictures professionally framed, set them about the house. It was probably pleasing her, as well as tracing with wonder these organic forms, in bright sunlight—or the combination of all these that made the painting work for me like a cure. It was an activity that had brought me close to nature, to my own mother. I was using it that summer to help me with the impending loss of my daughter, to heal me, to help me see things as they are and ought to be. Perhaps, finally, the work had done its job.

There was one thing I wanted to say to Anya, in our long talks about the future and what a woman should do and how to map her life, and what kind of love she needs. It went something like this: there is our inheritance, and then there is our essential essence, our own story. Much of our early adult lives we are dealing with messages that are really just the voices of our parents: roads not taken, the extreme importance of this or that aspect of things—in my past the emphasis was on physical beauty, achievement, financial security. Because we want to make our parents whole, to heal them, to please them, or to infuriate them, we take on these unfinished legacies and beliefs; or we rebel against them, striking out. There are other voices—what we should be doing, what we are really about. Often for years these are drowned out by the loud inheritance. I wanted to tell Anya: my problems are stupid, I know this. My problems were handed over, obstinate and seemingly everlasting, from my mother to me because her mother had some ridiculous notions which were some sort of rebellion against my grandmother's own limited pre-feminist universe, which in turn she inherited, backwards and backwards, forever. I actually felt like giving Anya a list of things that are the matter with me that *don't really matter* and shouldn't bother her, or shape her. The trouble, of course, is that we identify with these burdens. The trouble, of course, is that we want to make our parents happy. The trouble, of course, is that we love them terribly. Whatever list I might have given her, would just have been another voice from me; she will still have to sort all these out for herself.

On the bus, when we were coming into New York that last trip, I saw my face in the window and was disappointed, as usual, as always, with my looks. I started fiddling, as was my custom, with last minute beauty preparations. A slapdash attitude toward my appearance is an old rebellion against my mother whose toilette took hours, took on the importance of some solemn ritual: the preparation of the Shabbat table, say, or even a Catholic mass.

Anya criticized me, and took away my lipstick, my eyebrow pencil. She got out her own mascara. But she didn't just give me grief, as she had for years. She turned around and made up my face, very well, without going overboard. *I'm so happy, I can die right now,* I was thinking as she worked on my lashes.

This act was more intimate than a kiss, more complete. It was as if she had accepted some of my flaws now: she knew I was always careless in these matters and that was okay, she would deal with it. It was also as if she were saying: hereafter, you do it, go ahead: it's not that hard. Grow up, Mother. I can't spend my life fixing you up. This was a one-time thing. But she had turned back around. As if she were saying, with the eyebrow pencil, *I do see you, I do love you, but I have to go.* What she said was, "You look pretty, Mom," and then the bus merged left, to take on the Holland tunnel.

Barbara Selfridge.
A Note in Green Ink on Blue Paper.
Photographs.

NONIE SELFRIDGE SPARKS

A Note in Green Ink on Blue Paper Carried in My Purse for Over 30 Years

Dear Barbara,

I have a terrible unfinished feeling about saying goodbye last night. "Goodbye. I love you. I'm terribly terribly proud of you. You are the loveliest soda jerk I've ever seen. I do hope things go well on your trial. Remember John & Bob will both lend you money. And no matter how things go—life imprisonment, ten years probation, or whatever—please don't let it ruin your life. Just milk the experience for whatever it is worth, and remember you are a lovable worthwhile talented person."

If the plane crashes, Danaher has our will. Dickie is listed as guardian with you as alternate. Money about $200,000 goes into a trustfund with Bank of America & stays there until Peter is 25 & Margaret is dead. Now I've convinced myself that the plane *will* crash!

You are the best thing in my life—so far.

Mommy

Nonie Selfridge Sparks (1925-2001) was an early programmer on SWAC, the '50s computer located at UCLA. She and her two daughters were the toast of those early nerds, including John Selfridge, her mathematician first husband, and Bob Sparks, her crystalographer second husband.

In this 1972 note to me, her second daughter, John is my father, Bob my stepfather, Danaher the lawyer, Dickie my aunt, Peter at three my youngest half-sibling, Margaret my brain-damaged older sister. I was a student at UC Berkeley, up on a felony charge of battery on an officer after a chaotic campus-worker-support demonstration. I think my mother and step-father were flying to China for him to meet with other crystalographers (in '72?), and they'd brought the three kids up from Palo Alto to see me at my job before they left.

—Barbara Selfridge

DEEDEE AGEE

Body Language

We were bitterly estranged my mother and I, had seen each other only three times in thirteen years (one of those times was in court) when her best friend Mary phoned to say my mother had been asking for me.

"All night she was calling 'Teresa,'" Mary said. The name I'd gone by in grammar school, though Deedee had always been my family name. "Better come soon if you've a notion to see her." All the years of accusation, resentment, fury, betrayal and violent rejection didn't raise the thought not to go.

Everything in the house on King Street seemed uncannily smaller the way it had when I'd come home from being away at camp all summer. Mary, who'd taken care of things always, let me in, a dish towel in hand. "She's set up in the back room."

My mother lay in a hospital bed cranked part way up, so huge it took up most of the floor space in that room where we'd eaten dinner at the cracked milk glass and teak table (gone now), the room where, after my father died, my mother slept on a platform bed with drawers underneath that she stuffed her blankets into so the bed became a couch during the day. It surprised me that she still looked like herself. Despite the ravages of illness and her close-ness to death, skull pressing out against bluish gray skin, cheeks and temples hollowed, wisps of white hair sprouting here and there, blue veins mapping her scalp, my mother's face was still the one I'd always known, the one I once loved beyond all reason.

The "back room" was next to the "front room" where we set up the Christmas tree, where my parents played four hands on the piano and poker on Friday nights, where my father wrote all night on his wide carriage Underwood set up on the white Formica coffee table in front of the scratchy black couch and gave me sips of his scotch when I'd wake up in the night. Front room, back room. I was surprised then and am even now at the sheer power of the words to whisk me back in time and space, to tie me to my childhood self, to disclose how irrevocably a part of this family I still am.

My mother's head rested on the pillow like a cut jewel on satin, her eyes closed. Her earlobes hung down like the Buddha's. As a child, she was my object of desire, though she never seemed to have understood my longing, nor recognized that her body belonged to me. I'd trace the bulging veins on the backs of her hands with a fingertip. I'd push on them, trying unsuccessfully to make the plump blue worms lie flat, and then she'd hold her hands up in front of her face, fingers spread, and magically they'd disappear. I loved to smooth the billowing swoop of hair held back from her forehead by tortoise shell combs. On the sly I'd gently pummel the pillowy belly and breasts as she lay beside me telling bedtime stories about Carrot Top, a red-headed giant, good-hearted but dumb, and the two brilliant grasshoppers who lived in his ears and guided him out of one fix after another.

"Stop that," she'd say. When she'd fall asleep in mid-sentence, her voice trailing off first into nonsense, then silence, secretly, ever so gently, I'd bounce the jiggly, plumped-up bulge of flesh that overflowed the top of her brassiere.

The room was eerily quiet, the usual traffic noise muted. There was an oxygen clip in her nose. On her neck I noticed some of those dangly brown moles – "witches tits" she always called them. She'd have me take a piece of thread and tie them off at the base to make them dry up and fall off.

Her arms, veined and bony, lay outside the sheet. Her body seemed strangely flattened like a cartoon figure run over by a steam roller. I knew that she'd lost both breasts, but the flatness had to do with more than that, with something other. A coiled IV tube was taped to her left wrist, a catheter tube peeked out from beneath the covers and disappeared again behind the bedclothes. In a flash I understood: my mother was disappearing.

She opened her eyes then, her head rolling slightly in my direction, her eyes as pale blue as I remembered them, and I saw she knew me.

"Mother," I said. I walked closer to the bed. Her eyes stayed on me. I thought of her on the witness stand looking down, testifying on my estranged husband's behalf against my having custody of our son. At that time I still lived with the group of people I'd left home to be with, the group she considered a cult but which I saw as the only family I could depend on. I would never know whether it was my mother's testimony that was the deciding factor in my losing custody of my first child.

"It's me—Deedee. I came to see you."

"So I see." I couldn't read her, didn't know if she was glad or irritated, perhaps contemptuously amused.

I picked up her hand, dry and fragile as a leaf, perched on the edge of the high bed beside the outline of her legs, and leaned closer. My youth, my fertility, my robust health, seemed almost obscene to me. I flashed on times when as a teenager, reveling in my newly-discovered sexual magnetism, I'd come home with some new boy (or man—they were always much older), and sit around the kitchen table with my mother, and she and he would talk on into the night about art, aesthetics, philosophy, politics, on a level way over my head, and I'd feel out of it, stupid really. Later I'd take the guy to my room to make out and he'd always say at some point how lucky I was to have such a mother, so intelligent, knowledge-able and understanding, and it was as though I was the body, my mother the mind.

I looked down at her limp hand, so familiar, so like my own. Her eyes never left my face.

"So," I said into the silence. "How are you, mother?"

She stared at me, her mouth gathering into a line. "Not very good, obviously." She spat the words out through clenched teeth.

I felt instantly stupid, caught in a moment of what my mother would label as polite phoniness. There seemed to be nothing I could do with my face or hands or voice or body that would be a genuine gesture of myself in that moment. I was frozen stiff, a state so deeply familiar it seemed somehow true or right.

"I'm sorry," I said. "Are you in a lot of pain?"

"Not especially." She sniffed. Silence.

"Well, Mary called and said you'd asked for me."

She shifted her head. "So, what are you up to these days?"

I told her about my job as a chef at the Ballroom, a cabaret on West Broadway, how we plated up 78 covers for each show in about an hour moving at top speed in the semi-open kitchen, then prepped for the next seating in dead silence while the show was going on so as not to ruin the performance. I told her about the building I bought with friends, how we gutted the whole thing and dug out the five-and-a-half-foot-high basement—lugged the dirt up a ramp in pails—so we could stand up in it, turned it into a fantastic playroom for the kids many of us are starting to have, and how I love my room, which, though small, is light and pretty and filled with plants. Everything I said sounded phony in my ears, as though I was acting in a play and someone else was writing the script as I spoke. I told her about her grandson whom she's never asked to meet, who's two already, how he loves to build elaborate ramps and garages for his trucks and cars, who makes amazing paintings in daycare, who is in love with Felix the cat and carries a stuffed animal version of him around everywhere. He loves Miss Piggy too and wears only pink sweat pants and sweatshirts, pink velcro sneakers even.

She stared at me. I felt like a person trying to impress on a first date. I was trying so hard to please I hated myself. My efforts made me think of aborigines being photographed, sure the whole time their souls were being stolen.

I stopped chattering and we sat in tense silence. I was about to tell her the most real thing I could think of: that I was five months pregnant, that it was a boy, that I planned to name him Shane. The words had formed up in a line in my throat, but just then my mother gathered herself up and dropped my hand, pulled hers free and reached towards a glass of water amidst the pill bottles on her bedside table. Seeing the effort was too much for her I picked up the glass and leaned in to give her a sip. She turned her head away with a snap, the look in her eyes venomous, and called over her shoulder.

"Teresa," she rasped

I wasn't sure I'd heard her right.

"Teresa," she called again. I wondered if suddenly she'd forgotten who I was.

The door between the back room and the front room slid open then and a short black woman in white, a winged cap perched on her head, floated in.

"OK, Missus, don't you worry yourself none now." She looked at a wrist watch pinned to the lapel of her uniform. "Still a teensy bit early for your meds, dear."

My mother flapped her hand in dismissal. "Water," she whispered. The nurse took the glass from me and held it to the line of my mother's lips dribbling a little water into her mouth. My mother fell back against the pillows with a sigh.

"Thank you, Teresa," she murmured. "My guardian angel."

"Don't go an' tire yourself out now, Missus. Your daughter's here! Isn't that wonderful!"

My mother wasn't looking at me anymore. "I'm tired," she said. "Too tired for words."

I watched coldness spread inside me, a speeded-up film strip of a lake freezing. I wrapped myself around the words backed up in my throat that would never be spoken, my secret.

"Maybe I should go."

"Perhaps a little nap," said the nurse. She adjusted the clip on my mother's IV. "A short nap can work wonders."

But my mother shook her head. It was clear she wanted me to leave. I put my hand on her foot and squeezed gently. "I know you're tired, Mother," I said. "I'll let you rest." Her eyes were already closed.

Mary was standing in front of the refrigerator with a pencil filling in the grid of what looked like a schedule in her precise hand.

"She's got round-the-clock care now," she said. "So many different ones it's hard to keep track."

134

I couldn't bring myself to tell her the nurse's name.

Walking up Sixth Avenue, the filmy cotton of my Indian print skirt caressing my legs, I began to breathe again. Warmth spread out through me from a central core. I sat on a bench in Washington Square my hands around the gentle bulge of my belly, my secret, my self.

It was the last time I saw my mother. She died several weeks later on Independence Day. My son was born the following November. A few years later I came to see that my mother was right about the group I lived with, that it had become cult-like, and after a struggle, I moved out and on to a new life.

My youngest son is nineteen now. The veins pop out on the backs of my hands, blue worms beneath the surface. I remember how as a child he pushed down on them trying to make them disappear. Glancing at him, I'm surprised by the blue of my mother's eyes, looking back at me, warmed by love.

ALLISON JOSEPH

MY POSTHUMOUS MOTHER

She likes that I have a state job, well-paying,
even if the state isn't New York. Working
for the city, any city, is just too hard,
too few benefits for the work.

She likes that I'm married, even if
my husband isn't black, not Caribbean,
wonders when we're going to stop
fooling around, get down to the business
and make her some grandbabies—
half-white, half-black, she doesn't care.

Disappointed that I don't go to church,
or read the Bible, or think of Jesus,
she'd trade a few textbooks for hymnbooks,
wants me to pray more, put my palms
together, lift my face to the Lord.

Always a bargain lover, she's glad to hear
what we paid for this house, likes that
I put money away in savings, never touch it,
letting interest accrue on cash in case
of catastrophe, illness, death.

She's sad that I don't vacuum more, dust
more, that I let crusty dishes settle
in the sink for days, that I have forgotten
everything I might have learned
watching her at the stove, her hands
busy with chicken, rice, peas, water,
callaloo, yams—whatever made the house
fragrant. Sad to see me eat out so much,

she says she'd rather see me cook up
a savory meal of rice and pigeon peas,
pan of stewed chicken, meat
so soft it falls from the bone,
marrow ready to be sucked.

She likes hearing about my students—
their excuses, dramas, little victories.
Patients, students—not much difference
in her view—her hospitals and my
universities both needed to sustain us all.

She reminds me to go to the doctor,
take my vitamin, carry tissues in my
purse, to have spare change for the bus
or subway, to walk with my umbrella
on overcast days, keep two pairs of gloves
in winter, to try to learn to drive,
though she never did. *Wake each day
grateful*, she says, *for what you have.*
I wake each day glad to have been
her child, sorry that I cannot bring her
a cup brimming with warm tea,
a little sugar and milk making it
sweet enough to start the day.

ROCHELLE RATNER

Respecting the Weather

as you might respect,
not your mother,
but your best friend's mother

so that you leave home
with a jacket flung
over your shoulders
but return with it
neatly zipped

Pity the poor TV weatherman
giving equally futile warnings
equally anxious to help
(during blizzards and floods
he's on call around the clock)

But respect for the weather
is more than this

it's that slight pain arthritics
feel in their bones when it rains,
the headaches that set in
before any cold front,
it's knowing what mother wants
before she reminds you

Years after her death
you find yourself
filling your pockets with kleenex,
wrapping a scarf twice around your neck,
and closing her coat around you.

JANICE EIDUS

LIKE LOVERS

The windows of my mother's spare, antiseptic room in this prestigious Manhattan hospital look out on Central Park: the trees are bare but the air is balmy in late February, and people walk hatless and gloveless, their light jackets casually unbuttoned. But she, so frail in her loose hospital gown, her collarbones jutting out like two sharp stones, isn't looking out her window. Instead, she stares fixedly at me, squinting through her bifocals.

I sit across from her in a narrow metal folding chair that's wreaking havoc on my lower back. Sitting up tall, the way my yoga teacher has taught me to, I focus on my breath: inhale slowly, exhale slowly, inhale, exhale...

"I didn't like that other place at all," my mother says suddenly. Her voice is ragged and hoarse—a result of having been intubated for two weeks in the Intensive Care Unit of a Bronx hospital, before being moved here. "In that other place," she goes on, "the doctors robbed me and stole my pants, and then they left me in a bawdy house." Her eyes are wide, her expression a combination of outrage and bewilderment. "And then you came to see me, Janice," she says, "wearing a gold lamé suit and an Afro wig."

Giving up my attempts at perfect posture and breath control, I slump down in the unforgiving metal chair, feeling stunned at how rapidly, due to her sudden illness, she moves in and out of lucidity. I stare at her arms, legs, and hands, all grotesquely swollen from water retention, while the rest of her has shrunk. Her silvery hair is matted, and her skin, usually so glowing it makes her look ten years younger than her age of 79, is sallow. Each time she moves even slightly, she cries out in pain.

Just three weeks before, my mother spent the day on Fifth Avenue, doing things she loves: sitting on a bench at the fountain at Trump Plaza; reading magazines in the Donnell Library; stopping to use

139

the Ladies Room at Lord & Taylor's, her favorite public restroom in the city because, as she's told me many times, "It's roomy and clean and nobody bothers you." Then back home on the express bus to the Bronx, where she eats a typically light dinner of steamed fish and unbuttered bread (no vegetables because they don't agree with her), and goes to bed.

But in the middle of the night her bladder begins to burn, waking her. A urinary tract infection, she figures. She's had them before, and she isn't worried. She'll call her doctor the next afternoon if she's not better. But the hours pass, and her bladder burns and burns. She feels feverish. She can't sleep. The sun comes up. She's hot and sweaty, then chilled. Her bladder is on fire. Although she's beginning to hallucinate, she manages to call 911. Then she calls me, and in a slurred voice, leaves a message on my answering machine: "I'm feverish, I'm shaking, I'm waiting for an ambulance, I'm sorry."

But I'm not home, I'm swimming at my health club near Lincoln Center. I finish my swim, blow-dry my hair, dress, apply mascara and my latest acquisition in lipstick, a dark violet color I love. Then I treat myself to an especially nice lunch at a French café: pumpkin soup garnished with sunflower seeds, garlic bread, and a crisp salad. While I eat, I read a couple of my writing students' short stories. When I finish, I head downstairs to the restaurant's pay phone to check my machine for messages.

Two hours later, my husband, my brother, and I are all in the Bronx at her bedside in the ICU, where she lies connected to a variety of machines. Her urinary tract infection is tenacious, rapidly coursing through her bloodstream, shutting down her kidneys and other vital organs, rendering her body septic. Her blood cells can't extract sufficient oxygen. "She has less than 48 hours," the doctors tell us, "so prepare for the worst." They add, "It's a completely freak thing."

She hangs on. One day, two days, three. A tube is placed down her throat; her swollen hands ooze a thick pus that drips to the floor. "Mommy," I implore, as I stand at her bedside, "squeeze my hand to show me you know I'm here." Squeeze. "Mommy, nothing bad will happen to you. I'm here now. I'm taking care of you." Squeeze. Squeeze. Squeeze. Her eyes are wide, frightened; they follow me around the room.

In this cramped, curtained-off space in the ICU, I feel terrified. Terrified by my sudden, intimate knowledge of her frailty and mortality, and terrified by her sudden dependence on me. She and I have had a difficult relationship, with long periods of not speaking, and fierce arguments during those periods when we are speaking. Among other things, I've resented her dismissiveness of my writing, and she's been furious that I've chosen not to have children. "Being a writer without children is no life," she says. "You should stop writing." But right now our troubled history doesn't matter at all. Right now, more than anything else in the world, I want her to live.

Although the doctors pump a variety of antibiotics into her veins, her blood pressure drops precipitously. After a week, in a final attempt to save her life, without consulting me or my brother, they give her Livafed, a drug I've never heard of.

Livafed works by driving all the body's blood toward the heart and brain; unfortunately, gangrene of the extremities is an inevitable side effect. "Your mother is so lucky," one of the doctors tells me later, seemingly oblivious to the pain his words might evoke in me, "since only her fingers are gangrenous, not her entire hands. That means we'll only have to amputate her fingers." I'm in too much shock to do anything but nod as he walks away. Still reeling from his words, I head downstairs to the lobby for a cup of coffee. While fumbling for change at the coffee machine, I run into another of my mother's doctors, an Israeli woman with black hair to her waist. Casually, she says, "If your mother survives, her brain will be permanently out to lunch." Staring at her, once again all I can do is nod. But hours later, at home, I weep, wondering if it would have been better for her—and for me—if she had died. And wondering what choice I would

141

have made, had I been given a choice.

My mother remains in the Bronx ICU for another week and a half, now fully conscious and enraged by her situation. With the tube down her throat, her face a distorted mask of pain, the fear in her eyes a constant, she mimes repeatedly for me to pull out the tube. With her destroyed fingers, she writes barely legible notes on a notepad I bring her. "Get me out of here," she scrawls, "I beg you!"

And then one day on her own, when nobody is looking, she finds the strength to violently yank the tube from her own throat, despite her doctors' repeated warnings that she won't be able to breathe without it, and that she might damage her windpipe if she pulls it out on her own. But she's able to breathe, and her windpipe is unscathed. That same day, the doctors finally grant me permission to transfer her to this hospital in Manhattan, which I want to do for two reasons: it has a better reputation, and it's closer to my apartment. I'm so exhausted from standing at her bedside for hours each day—there are no chairs available for visitors in the ICU—and the bumpy, hot, stop-and-start hour-and-a-half bus trip to and from the Bronx adds to my exhaustion.

By the beginning of her second week in the new hospital, she's less grateful about being moved from "that other place." Now she's irritable and depressed. "Give me a lethal injection!" she demands of me in her hoarse, grating voice. "You're the one who did this to me; you're the one who let them give me that drug, so now end it!"

I keep my voice soft: "Mom, you're going to be okay. The doctors know what they're doing." I don't necessarily believe this, but it seems the right thing to say.

She frowns, and two things become clear to me: she's not placated by my words, and I'm going to bear the brunt of her anger from here on, since my brother has had to return to his full-time job, and I, with a more flexible schedule, am now the one in charge. I'm not thrilled with this arrangement—I've heard many times that it's usually the daughter, the female child, who ends up as the caretaker of aging parents. But I don't feel as though I have a choice.

Although my jobs as writer and teacher are just as demanding as my brother's office job, I have no employer who'll fire me. The truth is that I can stop writing for a while, which is exactly what's happening, and I can rearrange my private students' schedules. It's also true that when I'm not writing, I grow profoundly depressed, and I feel barely alive—something my mother has never understood.

At the end of the second week, the team of five doctors assigned to her case—all men with smudged eyeglasses—announces that the full length of her fingers won't be amputated after all. "We'll only need to amputate her fingers to the first knuckle," they say cheerfully. A few days later, a group of them gather around her bed. They've changed their minds again. "We've decided to opt for 'self-amputation,'" the head of the team says matter of factly to me, ignoring my mother who's staring up at him, her expression grim.

"Meaning what?" I ask, shifting uncomfortably in the rigid metal chair, not sure I really want to know.

"Meaning," he replies sternly, looking at me through eyeglasses so smudged his eyes are nearly obscured, "we're going to let her fingertips slowly fall off on their own." He, like most of the other doctors I've dealt with, seems oblivious to the impact his words might have on me. "At her age," he adds, still ignoring her and speaking sternly to me, "this is preferable to surgery."

Maybe so, I think, but I'm sickened by the thought of her having to watch deadened pieces of her own flesh disintegrate and fall away.

"Mrs. Eidus," a young blond doctor addresses her in a hearty, booming voice, "you should be very grateful that you're not losing your entire hands!"

She peers up at him through her bifocals, and asks in that grating, hoarse whisper I'm still not used to, "How grateful do you expect me to be?"

Her third week in the Manhattan hospital, I develop a terrible cold. This is my first visit to her in three days. I'm mostly better, although I'm still sniffling. Seeing her again, I'm startled and terrified anew by her charred, twisted fingertips; her thighs still so elephantine from water retention; her skeletal arms.

I help her to blow her nose, and then to gargle with mouthwash which I don't dilute enough so that it burns her throat, making her irritable, and I feel guilty and stupid. I brush her teeth, comb her hair, go outside and shop for jello and sorbet at the local deli because they're the only foods soft enough for her to eat, and then I feed them to her, spoonful by spoonful.

After she eats, she sleeps for a while. When she awakens, she asks me to wash her hands. Carefully, I wash each of her pitiful blackened fingers with a washcloth, trying to will the life from my own healthy fingertips into her rough, dead flesh.

The next day, the hospital staff announces that my mother will soon be ready to move to the rehabilitation unit of an Upper West Side nursing home. This will be a temporary move, for about a month. There, she'll be helped to become strong enough to walk again on her own; in the two months since she fell ill, she's become so weak she can't even sit up without help. She'll also be taught how to use her hands in new ways. But one of the crueler nurses frightens her when I'm out of the room. "The staff is very firm at the rehab unit," she tells my mother. "They won't help you to do anything, not a thing."

"It sounds like a concentration camp," my mother later says to me, her voice still hoarse, although less than before. Her eyes are frightened. "I'll do everything I can to cooperate. But what if they throw me out on the street?"

"Nobody will ever throw you out on the street," I say, wondering whether I should find this nurse and give her a piece of my mind for scaring my mother like this. But I'm tired of constantly arguing with hospital staff: they won't let her use her own pillow, and yet I have to argue with them for days until someone finds her a more comfortable pillow; the freezer in the tiny refrigerator in her room isn't large enough to hold even one container of the soft sorbet she needs, and it takes a full week of meetings and phone calls before I'm able to persuade them to move a larger refrigerator into her room—a task which takes them ten minutes.

Besides, I've got bigger worries at the moment than chastising some stressed out, overworked nurse. I'm worried about where my mother will live after she's discharged from the rehab unit. The doctors say because she's not chronically ill, she's not eligible for a nursing home, and yet she won't be strong enough—or able enough—to return to the Bronx apartment where she's lived alone since my father's death four years ago. I call an "Independent Living Facility for Seniors" on the Upper West Side, one I've seen advertised in a neighborhood newspaper. "In order to be eligible to live here," the woman on the phone tells me, carefully enunciating each word, "your mother has to be able to walk without assistance, and to carry her own tray of food to her table in the dining room."

My heart sinks: my mother is currently in a wheelchair, and as for carrying a tray on her own, who knows if she'll ever be able to do that without her fingertips? So I call the few assisted living facilities in the city. The requirements for assisted living aren't as strict as for so-called "independent living," but they're prohibitively expensive, between four and six thousand dollars a month. A couple of them, which are more affordable, are filled up and have closed their waiting lists. "There won't be a room for your mother," the administrator at a well-known facility tells me flatly, "in your lifetime."

On the day my mother is to be transferred to the rehab center of the nursing home, the ambulance is three hours late, and she grows so panicked she can't breathe and begins to cry, wiping her eyes with her damaged fingertips. Finally, the ambulance arrives and we speed through traffic. But before I can help her to settle into her new room, I'm given mounds of paperwork to fill out, and she and I are put through a series of seemingly endless meetings with doctors, nurses, administrators, social workers, and physical and occupational therapists.

But at last she's settled in, and it's Day Two, ten weeks after she first got sick. It's springtime now, but I'm so worn out that I've hardly noticed the change of seasons. My mother is having her first session with Layla, a physical therapist from the Philippines with waist-length, glossy black hair. Layla is kind and patient as she instructs my mother to wiggle her fingers and touch her nose. Next, she asks my mother to remove the big red "moon boots" she wears on her swollen, ulcerated feet, in order to do a series of ankle exercises. My mother surprises me by handling all these tasks with aplomb.

Outside her room I speak with her new doctor, a chubby pug-nosed woman wearing a surprising amount of gold jewelry. I ask her when she thinks my mother will be able to carry a tray of food, so that she can move into the independent living facility. "Maybe in two years," she says, doubtfully, shaking her head, "with the aid of some prosthetic devices attached to her hands. And maybe not even then." Now I'm really scared. Where will my mother live? Neither my husband and I, nor my brother, have space in our Manhattan apartments to take her in. Nor could I bear living with her day by day.

The next morning, the social worker from the rehab unit calls me. Her voice is sharp: my mother, with her clumsy hands, has spilled food on her nightgown and robe, and she has no change of clothes. This is my fault, the social worker implies: why hadn't I brought more of her clothes with her? But after seeing her only in hospital gowns for so long, it hadn't even occurred to me that here she'd need a full wardrobe.

The social worker's voice grows sharper as she pressures me to immediately go to my mother's apartment to get her clothes. But I honestly believe that I'll collapse if I don't have one day to recuperate. I refuse to go until the next day, and I don't care what the social worker thinks of me. My back is aching, I want to do

146

yoga, and after that, I want to rent a video—something light and frothy—and watch it with my husband. I call my therapist on the phone, whom I haven't seen since my mother got sick, and she tells me that I'm right to give myself a day off, that I deserve a little mothering myself. And that night as I sit close to John on our sofa, watching a movie, I devour two overflowing bowls of chocolate fudge ice cream.

The next day I head up to the Bronx with a two-page list of the clothes she'll need (panties, bras, stretch pants, blouses that slip over her head so that she won't have to manipulate buttons and zippers, and on and on). I spend hours going through her crammed closets and bureaus. My back is in tight, hard knots as I fill three large suitcases and a duffel bag—so much stuff that I have to call a private taxi to take me back into Manhattan.

After she's been in the rehab unit a week, her voice is no longer hoarse, but she's still not herself mentally. I'm more and more frightened that the Israeli doctor's warning about her brain being "permanently out to lunch" may be true. Among other things, she's forgotten how to use a telephone. Sitting up in bed, wearing one of the loose fitting polyester dresses I've brought her, her weak body propped against the headboard, she randomly punches numbers and then grows angry that the people she calls don't pick up their phones. As calmly as I can, I remind her that people have specific, individually-assigned phone numbers. I write my own phone number on a bright yellow Post-it, pasting it to her phone. Still, she punches numbers with no apparent rhyme or reason. "There," she says triumphantly, "you see! It's not me." A sly look crosses her face. "It's the nurses here. They don't want me to call out. They've sabotaged my phone."

"You're just feeling anxious," I say. "Take a deep breath before you dial." Once again, my calm voice belies my panic: where is she going to live, with physical and mental impediments? Every single day, I make phone calls to the same few assisted living facilities just in case a room opens up—but so far no luck. As the days pass, I make these calls by rote, with no hope or optimism.

Week Three in the rehab unit: I visit her in the late afternoon. I spot her sitting alone in the large dining room, wearing a blue-and-white flowered robe, looking like a lost little girl. "The nurses are sabotaging my phone again," she says in greeting. "There's a major conspiracy against me."

"You're just not dialing correctly." I kiss her hello, and join her at her table. "There's nothing wrong with your phone."

Leaning forward, she says intensely, "I really do know that it's me and not the phone. But I feel so confused and angry and humiliated. And this place overwhelms me: so many nurses and aides all day and all night. Some of them yell at me, some are more tolerant, but I can't take it."

"I know." I try to sound reassuring. My heart overflows with love for her, for her ability at this moment to be so honest. I refuse to believe that her confusion is permanent.

She begins to giggle suddenly, a mischievous expression on her face. "I peeked at my occupational therapy chart," she says. "I'm doing great in all my physical exercises. But they wrote in big letters: Mentally Confused."

"But you know, the fact that you know it and recognize it, is a great sign. People who are really confused don't know it." I'm not certain that this is true, but I hope it is.

"That's right," she agrees, touching her head. "Those people are all gone up here. I'm only part gone." She pauses, then speaks softly. "And thank you, Janice, for everything you've done for me. I'm aware of your sacrifices."

"You're welcome," I say, taking her marred hand in mine, realizing how much I've wanted to hear these words.

Finally, after weeks of fruitless phone calls, a room becomes available at one of the relatively affordable assisted living facilities. As I make arrangements to bring my mother in for an interview, I try not to dwell on the fact that probably someone has died, making this room so suddenly and unexpectedly available.

A few days later, I take two Motrin for my back, and with great difficulty, I manage to get her into a cab and across town to the east side to meet with the director of the facility. A stale smell permeates the drab halls and lobby, and the creaking, claustrophobic elevator is ancient. We're ushered into a tiny office with peeling walls, where we meet Greg, the director, and Bob, the social worker. Almost immediately, they begin their assessment of my mother. Bob is thin and young, with a wispy goatee. He asks my mother to describe her illness.

"I'm a miracle," she says proudly, holding up her mangled hands as evidence. "I wasn't supposed to live."

Bob looks at her hands, then down at the floor. "Mrs. Eidus," he asks, still not looking at her, "do you have any significant others?"

My mother's expression is blank.

Stroking his insubstantial goatee, he looks up. "Do you have any lovers?" he asks.

"Janice is my lover," she answers blithely.

Embarrassed, I look away, but not before I see Bob and Greg exchange small smiles. I'm not as amused as they are, however, because I know that she's right. There's nobody on this earth who loves her more than I, even if my love is colored by years of anger and disappointment and feelings of betrayal. Whether I like it or not, I have become her lover.

"How is your hearing, Mrs. Eidus?" Greg, the burly, flannel-shirted director asks, thankfully changing the subject.

"It's okay," she says, "except I have trouble understanding Fran Drescher on *The Nanny*." She giggles, seeming to know how cute and charming she's being.

Greg nods, exchanges another small smile with Bob, and continues. "Mrs. Eidus, do you know where you are right now?"

"Yes," she says, promptly naming another assisted living facility a few blocks away, one that's much more expensive and well-appointed. Now all of us, except my mother, appear embarrassed.

The next morning I call Greg, who cheerfully informs me that she's been accepted: in two weeks, when her time at the rehab center is over, she'll have a new home. I want to weep with gratitude, even though I now face the overwhelming task of closing out her cluttered apartment of 25 years.

That afternoon, I return alone to the assisted living facility to fill out paperwork and to leave a deposit. Bob, the social worker, says, "You know, you're absolutely instrumental in her miraculous recovery. Not all children are so involved, so close to their mothers, believe me." I'm stunned, and I want to protest, to tell him that she and I have never been particularly close before now, and that what is happening between us surely won't last. It's just another symptom of her acute illness, I'll explain: before too long, all the old angers and grudges will surface. But I force myself to say nothing, accepting the compliment.

My mother's first full day at the assisted living facility is a disaster: the aide I've hired doesn't show. Luckily, an aide working with another resident on my mother's floor needs extra money and is eager to help. But the instant she and I walk in to my mother's room, my mother shouts, "Bring me my credit card at once, Janice!" She begins to weep. "I can't live like this, here in this senile place. I'm not who I was!" She becomes incontinent, soiling herself—a recurrent problem since the onset of this illness—and continues to weep as the hastily-gotten aide cleans her.

I go out for a lunch break. When I return, she's been cleaned up and is wearing a pair of pink culottes and a jersey top. Imperiously, she says, "Bring me a loaf of bread, 50 styrofoam cups, six iced teas, and a phone with big buttons and speed dial." Grateful that she's not weeping any longer, I unquestioningly turn around and head back outside to do her bidding. In the elevator, I run into the head housekeeper, a Chinese woman with a dyed blonde bun. "I was afraid they make a mistake, accepting your mother, maybe she has no fingers, I think," she says in halting English, "but now I'm not worried. She's so smart. Do you know how smart she is?" "Yes," I reply, truthfully, "I do."

Back in my mother's room, I show her the bread, cups, and tea

150

that I've bought. John will bring the phone later. But she's angry that I haven't brought her credit card. "Look," I say, "just temporarily, while you're a bit like the child and I'm like the mother, maybe I should hold on to your credit card."

"No," she says, shaking her head, "bring it to me."

"Remember," I say, "how when I was a kid you used to be firm with me and say, 'No, you can't do that!' Well, I'm saying it now."

Very calmly, she answers, "And you never listened to me. You went ahead and did exactly what you wanted to, anyway."

This stops me in my tracks for a moment. "Okay," I say, laughing, "so let's just assume that I'm wiser than you were back then, and that, unlike you, I really do know best!"

She joins me in laughter at my hubris, and it's a good moment, the best moment we've had together in a while.

A few days later she calls to tell me that Bob, the goateed social worker, has paid her a visit to try to get her to "open up." "But I told him," she says, "that I don't want to talk about my physical state. It just makes me cry. And I don't want to cry. I've cried enough in my lifetime. I told him I'm a pragmatist who takes things moment by moment." Her voice grows loud and angry. "I told him I understand exactly what has happened to me and what I'm facing, and I only hope I have the fortitude to face it. And that was all I would say on that subject! What I really wanted to talk to him about was the way that the kitchen help here are so snippy to me. He said maybe I didn't understand that they're from the Middle East, a different culture. I said I do understand, but that I want a cup of tea in the middle of the night and they won't let me have it. But, okay, if they're not willing to make me tea when I need it, that's that. I won't complain again." Her voice has grown increasingly loud and strident. "So you have to understand, Janice, that I will drink as much ginger ale as I need to! I will not ration myself! Even if the ginger ale adds hundreds of dollars to my expenses."

It exhausts me to hear how angry and frightened she is. "Mom," I say, "nobody will ever stop you from drinking as much ginger ale as you want, I promise."

Suddenly she's conciliatory. "When my fingertips fall off," she says, "I'll try to learn to carry a tray so I can go to live in the more independent place."

The next day, I come home to a phone message from her: "I had a better night last night. I watched some TV and drank ginger ale." A second message is from my mother's nurse at the home: "One of your mother's fingertips just fell off!" she says. "This is great!"

Two days later, my mother and I are in a taxi en route to the vascular surgeon who will monitor her fingertips, as well as the two painful bed sores that have developed on her feet. Her finger is heavily bandaged, so I can't see where the tip fell off. "A lot of blood," is all she'll say about it. She stares out the cab window. "Once I enjoyed looking at buildings, at the outside world, but now I'm like a prisoner being released into the fresh air. It's just too late; I no longer care."

The vascular surgeon, who has an international reputation in his field, is French. He looks at my mother's hands: "You look like you're in a horror movie." He speaks coldly, in a beautiful accent that accentuates the cruelty of his words. I'm ready to punch him in the face, but my mother giggles and eyes him almost flirtatiously. He walks out of the room. My mother says to me, "This doctor is knowledgeable, and I like his personality a great deal." I decide not to say a word. He's her doctor, after all, not mine.

He returns and looks at the two large, oozing, ulcerated bedsores—"wounds," he calls them—on the heels of both of her feet. "Two months for the feet to heal," he says. "Six months for all the fingertips to fall off."

The following week we return. This time he says, "Five months for the feet to heal, and a year for the fingertips to fall off."

After he's finished cleaning her hands and feet, he leaves so she can dress. I start to put her elastic stockings back on her legs. "No," she snaps. "You're not careful enough! Get a nurse to do it."

"Mom," I say, as calmly as I can, "trust me, I can do it."

Efficiently, I pull the stockings up her swollen, heavily veined legs, and then I strap on her surgical shoes.

"You did very well," she proclaims regally, and I feel proud—and then angry at myself because her praise, never readily given, still means so much to me.

Two weeks later, we have a very bad day. One of her fingertips is swollen and infected. She's in great pain. I rush her to the vascular surgeon. "Don't worry," he says in his typically cold manner, barely glancing at her, his romantic French accent dissonant as always, "this will happen. Probably again and again."

And he's right, it does happen—again and again. As the weeks pass, her fingertips swell and ooze and bleed. She and I go back and forth to the vascular surgeon. We continue to wait for the rest of her fingertips to fall off, and for the sores on her feet to heal. I wait, too, to see whether her mental state will improve. Sometimes she uses the telephone correctly; sometimes she doesn't. Occasionally she still talks about being robbed and left in "bawdy houses." Throughout, she demands her credit card, but I still refuse to bring it to her.

But little by little, day by day, even as her lucidity waxes and wanes, she acclimates to her new living situation in "the senile place," as she insists on calling it. She no longer begs me for a lethal injection. Three times a week each, an occupational and physical therapist come to her room to work with her. Carla, the physical therapist, has a long, thick braid to the middle of her back, making her look like a '60s radical, which I suspect she was. My mother says that "Carla is like a daughter to me. I hug and kiss her whenever I see her." My mother's illness seems to have made her warmer, more open to others, and this pleases me. Still, I feel a bit miffed that a woman she's known for only a few weeks appears to have as much a place in her heart as I do.

After about eight weeks in "the senile place," her incontinence has mostly passed. One morning, she calls to say that—using her walker—she'd ventured outside by herself to a stationery store and bought a calendar in which to keep track of doctor's appointments. She also stopped at a deli to buy a six pack of ginger ale. I'm thrilled by how far she's come physically, and I'm also now certain that her brain isn't permanently out to lunch. In addition, her good looks have returned—her recently trimmed Buster Brown bob is flattering, and her skin is beginning to take on its normal tone.

But now that she's so alert, she's upset by the assisted living facility. "It's too sad here," she says, shuddering as she tells me about one tiny woman in her 90s who occasionally runs naked through the dining room, smearing her feces along the walls.

Then, on a cloudy February afternoon, a year since she first got sick, my mother calls me. "I can do it!" she shouts. "I've been practicing like I promised, and now I can carry a tray all by myself, so I'm ready to move to the independent place."

I'm as elated as she, and I immediately call the Independent Living Facility for Seniors, which is back across town on the west side, and soon we're being interviewed again. My mother now uses a cane when she walks, and this time there's no childish talk on her part about The Nanny or about me being her lover. This time she has just two concerns: being accepted, and getting a room with a view.

At the close of the interview, we're given a tour. There's no stale odor permeating the halls, and the building is brightly lit, with a glass-enclosed roof garden, a plushly-carpeted lobby, a smiling doorman, gift and coffee shops, and a decently-stocked library. The residents smile and greet one another, and I overhear conversations that people of any age might have—about the weather, about politics, about the guests the night before on The Tonight Show.

A few weeks later, we get a call letting us know that she's been accepted. But there's no room available, so we have to wait some more. Five weeks after that, a large room with a sweeping view of Broadway opens up. The woman who had been renting it, we are told, developed Alzheimer's shortly after moving in, and had to move to a nursing home.

It's a crisp day in November, and it's my birthday. It's also exactly one year and nine months since my mother's urinary tract infection landed her in the ICU in the Bronx. She and I are meeting for lunch at a Chinese restaurant uptown. She will walk the five blocks from the independent living facility to the restaurant by herself, without even using a cane. She'll walk slowly, it's true, stopping to catch her breath at every corner, but she'll be walking, and that's what counts. At lunch, she'll handle her knife and fork with dexterity, even pouring her own tea. Once or twice, she'll drop something and her hands will falter, but she'll quickly regain her poise.

Over our shared order of steamed chicken in white sauce, we argue just as we used to before she fell ill: she tells me that my writing isn't ever going to bring me fulfillment, and that only having a child will do that; I tell her that my life is as fulfilling as the lives of most people I know, mothers included. She insists that therapy isn't helping me, because if it were, I would have children; I suggest that she might benefit from some therapy herself, and she scoffs at the idea.

But we get through these arguments without either of us storming away from the table or flinging down her knife and fork in a rage. Instead, we move on to other subjects: she tells me in detail about her bus ride into midtown the week before when a nice young man gave her his seat. She describes a recent, happy foray into the clean, spacious Ladies Room at Lord & Taylor's. She asks about my back, and is pleased that I'm completely pain free. I tell her about the trip to Mexico that John and I are planning: where we'll stay, what we'll do, how we'll travel.

Truly, she and I have become like lovers of many years: intimately familiar with each other, accepting of our tempers and foibles. At the end of the meal, after I have finished my last cup of unsweetened, dark tea and she has downed the tall glass of ginger

155

ale she's been sipping slowly like an aperitif, she will pay for the lunch—it's her birthday present to me, after all—with her very own credit card.

BARBARA ZIMMERMANN

A LETTER TO MOTHER ON MOTHER'S DAY

May 13, 2001

Dear Mom,

In the forties, you were the woman in high-heeled pumps, gussied-up in a red jersey dress with a swingy hemline that revealed your shapely calves, and with long tapered fingers tipped with crimson polish. Your fur coat carried the scent of Tabu and after you had left for work, when I was four or so, I'd bury my nose in the soft fur and inhale the essence of you as if that would bring you back. In the fifties, then, you were the woman with ebony hair pulled back into a chignon and dusky blue eyes which either smiled promises of good times to your daughters or clouded over when a storm was brewing. Later, in the early sixties, you wore your hair short, in natural waves that framed your square-shaped face, and trousers and a sporty blouse became the staples of your wardrobe. Tabu, that musky, exotic scent, remained your signature, wafting through the room long after you'd departed.

You were the woman whose forefinger traced patterns over my forehead when I'd lay my head in your lap, seeking comfort; the woman who met me at the door when I came home from grade school, asking, "How was your day, baby?" In high school, you bought a prom dress for me at a rummage sale for fifty cents—a spaghetti strapped dress of white voile embroidered with pink roses and accented at the waist with a pink cummerbund. You convinced me that no one would ever know and I went to the junior prom in '59, feeling confident that my secondhand dress was as lovely as any new-bought. After I graduated in '60, you applauded my decision to skip college, hop a plane to Florida, and explore another world. When I called and asked if I could return home a scant six months later, you welcomed me back, no questions asked. At twenty, I moved again to Florida and felt the earth

157

quake beneath my feet when President Kennedy was assassinated. Though I heard concern in your voice when I called you on the phone two months later, you accepted my decision to hitch a ride to San Francisco where I thought I'd somehow reconcile my disillusionment in humankind and find the answers I was searching for "blowing in the wind."

On a wintry day in February of 1964, two weeks after my call to you from California, you were the forty-six-year-old woman who lay down on the couch at eleven in the morning—a copy of *Good Housekeeping* lying open on your chest, a Tupperware glass full of Kool-Aid laced with scotch on the coffee table, and hand laundry soaking in the kitchen sink—and suffered a massive cerebral hemorrhage. You were dead a few hours later. When I sat at the bar in the airport lounge waiting for the flight that would carry me from San Francisco to Indianapolis, I stared into the mirrored wall across from me and swore I saw your image: a blue-eyed, dark-haired woman wearing a white roll-up-sleeved blouse with khaki slacks, a black onyx ring on one finger of the right hand and a diamond studded wedding band on the ring finger of the left keeping time to "Alley Cat" blaring from the juke box.

Since the age of twenty-one, I've searched for you in the cologne counters of department stores, in the distant retreating figure of a woman near your age walking down the street, and in the Hallmark cards displayed each May. And occasionally, Mom, when the heart seeks what the mind cannot accept, I do find you during the quiet moments at night residing in that part of me that has clung to your memory for over thirty-seven years.

Love, Bobbi

LAUREN MCCOLLUM

MOTHER OF PEARL

This body you gave me is a shell, a home
my anima carries with it wherever it goes,

a shell, encasing the nut, the yolk, the animal within,
one sprung from the shelter of your womb.

These hips you gave me are mighty in a way
that boasts *I have swallowed a dinosaur's egg.*

The arc shoots boldly from my waist, a place
to rest your grandchildren and mine.

This breath you gave me is a brief fog,
the prize of a shell game sure to be lost at end.

Look, already it sighs away from you,
gasping its way into a metropolis,

its intent to fade
into the motherless flow.

RITA DOVE

EXIT

Just when hope withers, a reprieve is granted.
The door opens onto a street like in the movies,
clean of people, of cats. Except it is *your* street
you are leaving. Reprieve has been granted,
"provisionally"—a fearful word.

The windows you have closed behind
you are turning pink, doing what they do
every dawn. Here, it's grey: the door
to the taxicab waits. This suitcase,
the saddest object in the world.

Well, the world's open. And now through
the windshield the sky begins to blush,
as you did when your mother told you
what it took to be a woman in this life.

CECILIA WOLOCH

NEST

We didn't have anything, she says.
We were poor; everyone was poor back then…
No such thing as car seats for babies;
I just held you in my arms.
So I was new-born, it was Thanksgiving Day,
and probably swaddled in pink in the crook
of my mother's girlish arm.
And of course there would be no cradle
in my father's Teta's house.
We just opened a drawer, you were so small…
so they lay me down among linens, clothes—
a nest I'd remember if memory served
to keep us just this safe, this warm.

I talk to my mother over the phone
on a Spring day, thousands of miles from her.
I lean back in a shaft of sunlight, listen:
this is her voice, this is home.

JESSIE L. JANESHEK

FOR MY MOM: A BEACH RADISH, CUT DECORATIVELY

Currents jerk the seafruits
off their horizontal vines and trees.

Shrieks gurgle from the nurseries,
settle on the water,
on this piece of beach where

sea-orchards wash crops,
where I walk between aloe-green
rods, still throbbing.

Brown balls look like styrofoam
coconuts, thirst for milk.
You'd smile at the squat ones,

bloodied, pumpkinish. Their wine-maroon roots
splash above stems

like hands tossed in distress,
this whole dispersed salad

garnished with parts of purple shells
split as if they'd meet

to make the enchanted amulet
in a book you used to read me.

When two halves kiss, the moon
will lurch and turn, glittery

as a clog of damp salt.
I'll harvest this mess,

lonely ocean produce,

take it home to rinse.
Plop it in a silver pot, sauté

a recipe for medley,

except I'm not the great creator.
I'm just the hungry daughter.

J. PATRICE WHETSELL

THE COCONUT LADY

M y mother taught me to cook the summer before I went to college because she believed I would starve to death if left to rely on the services of the campus dining hall. "What you will eat? They nuh know how fe make rice and peas there," she would say. "You must learn to cook yourself."

I am not surprised my mother worried so much about my diet. She has always believed in the power of food, a necessity that, with a little ingenuity, can be made into a luxury, and is indispensable in the art of seduction. In her estimation, food is power to a woman, even more so than beauty "You will never find love until you learn to cook," she has often said. "True love is made in the mouth."

My mother holds three basic ideas about food: that it should be pleasing to the eye as well as to the palate, that it should be enjoyed, and that it should not be restricted to what is good for you, although those things good for you should be included when possible. She is a wonderful cook, her meals being inspired by whimsy rather than recipe, desire rather than diet. She never reads nutrition statistics and has never counted a calorie in her life.

We began with coconuts because they are the most difficult fruit and my mother's favorite, a secret weapon in almost all of her dishes. The first thing to do is to look at the "eyes" of the coconut, three small craters, distinguishable but partially concealed by hair. "Naked eyes, like eyes without lashes, no good," Mother warned. "Ignore them." She called them having poor sight. An experienced shopper will never shake a *poor-sight fruit*. A good ear is also necessary for choosing a coconut because you must shake it. A good coconut will be *full up* of water.

Every week we bought two coconuts, one to use in rice and peas and one to snack on. My mother inspected each coconut on the shelf, shaking her head and sucking her teeth as she picked the bad ones up and put them back. "So many gone bad by the time they get here, all dry up," she would say. But she always succeeded in finding some that looked decent.

Opinions differ as to the best way to crack open a coconut, but my mother believes in the virtue of simplicity. She cracks coconuts by throwing them against the ground. Maybe that practice wastes the milk, but some of my fondest memories are of me and my mother on the back patio, the sound of a hard shell smashing against concrete. If it was good, she would hold the coconut high above our heads, milk spilling everywhere, and the two of us dancing underneath, sticking out our tongues and lapping it up. Very often these coconuts were not good, though, and we would have to return them.

The first time my mother tried to return a coconut, the cashier stared open-mouthed at the woman pushing a sticky plastic bag of broken coconut, leaking milk and covered with hairs, toward him on the counter. "We can't take this back. It's open," he stammered. My mother said, "It's no good. I don't want it." The boy looked back and forth between my mother and the puddle of coconut milk now dripping slowly onto the floor. "Won't take it," my mother said. He called his manager and then maintenance for a cleanup.

That day my mother discovered it was easier to let the men in the grocery store open the coconuts. She took her 99 cents and went back to the produce aisle, chose another coconut and stopped an employee. "Open this for me, please?"

The man laughed while he talked. "Lady, I can't do that. You have to *buy* it first."

"I won't buy it first. It's bad, I just return it anyway, so you can just open it now." My mother handed him the coconut and he walked away.

The men at the grocery store make a hole in one eye to save the milk and let my mother taste it. She pauses and either shakes her head vehemently or nods languorously with pleasure, and we know instantly whether the fruit is worthy or not. That day the coconut was bad. My mother demanded that the man open another coconut, and another. I stood at her side, holding her hand and squirming in my shoes, whispering, "Let's go, Mama." She ignored me until finally all the coconuts in the store were sitting in the stockroom, broken and useless. My mother refused to pay for any of them. She thanked the man for his trouble and said simply, "Let's go home now." The next week when we went shopping, the man called out, "Hey, it's the Coconut Lady!" when he saw us. My ears burned red, but my mother only laughed.

My mother says that back home people would laugh to see us eating the dry coconut, only good for cooking with. In Jamaica coconuts grow large and hard and green. And when you cut one down and chop off the top there is a cream-colored fibrous layer inside, and then a layer of clear jelly you can eat with a spoon, and the coconut water you can drink with a straw. The brown, hairy coconuts we see in the grocery stores here are only the dried remains of those fresh green glories. But she would take a bite out of the dry coconut and laugh, and throw the rest into the blender to grind for her rice.

My second lesson was in selecting all other produce. This is easier because it only requires sight, smell, and touch. I had gone to the grocery store with her every Saturday since childhood, and in the spring and summer also to various farms. We spent hours on the weekend driving around to different markets so that she could buy fruits and vegetables at her favorite places.

My mother's words still echo in my ear. She has lost most of her Jamaican accent from twenty years in America, but I love the unique sounds she makes, how she sucks her teeth when she is unsatisfied, the way she enunciates all the letters of certain words like vegetables and Connecticut. Ve-ge-*te*-bels.

Fresh vegetables always when possible. Frozen, second choice. Canned only for certain recipes or emergencies. Tomatoes from Ann's farm, over on 22. Cucumbers, peppers, and squash from the Abbots on the east side. They grow plenty things, but they have the sense not to make them grow big and tasteless. Peaches from Glengarry Orchards.

166

Ed Burns's plums are the best. Strawberries and blueberries you can get in May, but raspberry season's not till July. Apples in the fall from Dell's. Gala sweet for snacking, Granny Smith, sour, and McIntosh, baking. Never buy anything that ends in Delicious. It's usually not. Use your thumb to buy pears—you should be able to press them in slightly near the stem. Apples should stay firm. Sniff melons.

Lettuces and all produce not grown in our area we bought at the local grocery store. Potatoes and onions individually, never bagged because too often they're sweaty, cabbages, mushrooms, bananas, avocados, mangoes. These can be red or green, bi- or tri-toned, even speckled when ripe. They're all still common mangoes, imported en masse to consumers who have never heard of guinea hens and don't know what they're missing—Julies and Bombays, East Indians and Saint Julians and Robins. I've often marveled at my mother's trading a dozen varieties of mangoes and a papaya tree in the backyard for three kinds of berries, hard-to-peel oranges, and pineapples that burn the roof of your mouth.

Presentation was the third lesson, color being the major principle. Salads are a good starting point for contrasts, and they're usually the first thing a guest will see.

Start with a dark green lettuce; the other vegetables show up better against it. Bright red tomatoes make a beautiful contrast; so do carrots. Red cabbage is good. There are few things that purple. Red onions for the same reason, and they're sweet too. But white or yellow ones for cooking. Always use fresh Vidalia when you can get them. Red peppers are good too, although yellow are more distinctive. A little fruit can go a long way in traditional salads. Like spinach salad with orange slices and mushrooms. Cantaloupe on Romaine.

You can make salads more interesting by mixing and matching flavors, textures, and shapes. Sweet and sour, crisp and soft, cubes and circles and shredded things.

And never underestimate the importance of table setting: flowers and tablecloths should complement the colors of the food as well as of the room it's being served in. White tablecloths are basic, and you can never really go wrong with them, especially on dark wood, but some-

times you want something more original. They're also good if you're serving dark dishes, like stews and chilis, or anything with a lot of different colors, although you have to be careful because these things stain. Gardenias are good for the same reason, but never against a white tablecloth unless you're trying to make some kind of statement. Gladiolas are always nice; any tall flower really, to add height. Yellow and purple go well together. Hyacinth is a lovely shade for curries. You can also go the other way and use daffodils with eggplant. Stuffed eggplant is best because it retains its royal color. Almost anything will liven up pale whites like stroganoffs and chicken. I like red flowers, but sometimes plain green plants are better. Never skimp and never buy store-made arrangements. Cheapness shows.

During the next few weeks, my mother taught me what size pots were best for making which dishes, how to use spices, and how to prepare the dishes I had been raised on—rice and peas, hominy, curried goat and chicken, jerked pork, ackee and saltfish, pepper-dash stew, fried plantains, gazottas.

On my last night home, my mother and I made dinner together. I started washing handfuls of gungu peas for rice and peas while she searched for the pressure cooker.

"You can soak the peas and cook them on the stove, but the pressure cooker's faster and it always make them soft. They never come out so soft on the stove," she said.

I nodded. I took out the other ingredients—white rice, coconut, onion, garlic, parsley, fresh thyme, and little rainbow-colored hot Scotch Bonnet peppers. My mother found the pressure cooker and started to boil water. Then she came over to see what I was doing. "How do you do the coconut, Mom?"

"Here, it's easy after you already have it broken up. Just take off the shell and grind it up."

Her arms moved quickly as she dug the coconut out of its shell with a knife and threw large pieces into the blender. We fell silent as the blender whizzed, turning the coconut into gray mush. I started to peel the onion and garlic on the table.

"Remember to mince it up. And chop those peppers tiny, too.

168

You don't want to burn him when he eats."

I grinned. "Who says there's going to be a him?"

She smiled knowingly. "You'll find a nice man at school."

"I'm not going to school to meet a man, Mom."

"I know. But lots of girls meet a man in college. And now you'll know how to cook well, you'll find a nice man. There's no secret to love. Just remember: live with the little things. No man is perfect. And neither are you."

"Is that how it is with you and Dad?"

"Put the rice on to boil while you finish that chopping. Use a sharper knife for the garlic—it will go faster. Here, let me do it."

Her wrist bobbed up and down rapidly as she chopped. Tiny pieces of garlic jumped in the air before landing in golden piles. I stopped chopping spices.

"He's never around anymore."

"You are."

"He doesn't eat your food anymore."

"You do."

"Who will eat it when I'm not here?"

She laughed. "Don't worry about me and your father. Besides, I'm tired of cooking every day. It will be nice to order out and eat TV dinners instead. I can just cook when I want to.

"We need something to go with this. You want to make ackee? Make sure you get all the bones out of the saltfish. They're tiny and I don't want anybody to choke."

She put the peas and spices into the pot with the rice. "Parsley last," she said. Then she joined me at the kitchen table, and we pulled bones out of the saltfish until the rice was cooked.

That night, as I was packing the last of my things, I noticed a small wrapped box in the corner of my suitcase. Inside was a bottle of Jamaican white rum and an apron with the words Coconut Lady embroidered in script across the top. There was also a small piece of white paper, folded several times. It read: *Always use pressure cooker for beans. The tall black pots for rice or stews. The red heavy one is good for chicken. Use the round green ones for cooking vegetables—that way they don't stick.*

There are certain things a kitchen must have—curry powder, onion and garlic, turmeric—for color and taste. Parsley, ginger because it goes well with coconut, basil, condensed milk, and honey. And a bottle of rum. It's nice to drink at night, plus it's good if you're getting sick. Never buy curry powder in a grocery store. Get a real Jamaican one. Cumin is nice too, and a dash of oregano goes a long way.

Curries are simple; you just need to make sure you have enough water in the pot to make a sauce. And curry will cover almost any mistake, unless you add too much; then you just make a new one. Buy good jerked seasoning same way you get curry powder. Stuff it in the pork. Remember to spread it evenly; you don't want to burn someone. Hominy is just corn and condensed milk, ginger, nutmeg. Do the corn in the pressure cooker. Fried plantains are easy, green and turning black is ripe. Better to use shortening than oil. Gazottas—just grind the coconut and boil it with sugar, a little ginger too if you want. Make your dough and fill it. Watch the oven because they burn fast, but they're best when they've browned. Sorrel we always make at Christmas, but it's good for any party. Bright red, very festive. Boil the sorrel leaves, strain the juice, and mix it with white rum. Everything else you must learn yourself.

PAULETTE ROESKE

Travel by Water

In the kitchen beside the warm stove
where the loaves of challah rise,
I turn to my daughter, rest my hands
on her belly, fingers splayed to hold her new heft,
the three of us, eyes closed against the day,
caught in an oceanic drift, sway
of sargassum weed or endless eelgrass bed.

Little seahorse, vertical swimmer,
nodder, fingerling, fellow traveler, child
of my child, I cross the crossable terrain—
one generation, the skin's open plain, deep tissue, water,
blood, and salt—to see with my fingers,
as I saw your mother before you,
you who will join the line of women who already
feels the ache of readiness in their arms.

Generation after generation they rise like tortoises
from the ancient sea, crowning
to offer their riches—horny plate, invaluable shell—
generations on whose backs you will walk to the end
of what I know: your great-great-grandmother, the first woman
in my memory, watched from the grave
as your mother clawed her way into the waking world,
proving the past is not ash
but flesh behind the veil. Child,
begin counting backwards,
turn down the years to reach
the industry of her embrace,
woman whose life I will tell you,
although you already know the story

of travel by water.

As for me, daily I search both sides
of the river, open to the press
of the dead and the unborn,
which is how I found you, my
long-lashed beauty, here
in this kitchen, beside the braided loaves,
warm, and ready to eat.

ALICIA OSTRIKER

MIKVAH

—with thanks to Phyllis Berman

late afternoon the august sun reddens
its power to heal us or scorch us wanes
we women undress on the grass

like flying-home exiles we greet our bodies
clasping hands praying dropping our towels
we climb into the hot tub

cedar smell water spark
in threes we immerse ourselves
like jewels fallen overboard we create

tiny splashes then the water quiets
fear loosens like flakes of dead skin
grief rises like steam

we immerse further
then we emerge breathe again
we speak in low voices

you join us
with our wet hair
each shyly having left some prayer down there

in the tireless flowing
out we climb
like showered robins

LUCILLE CLIFTON

FEBRUARY 13, 1980

twenty-one years of my life you have been
the lost color in my eye. my secret blindness,
all my seeings turned grey with your going.
mother, i have worn your name like a shield.
it has torn but protected me all these years,
now even your absence comes of age.
i put on a dress called woman for this day
but i am not grown away from you
whatever i say.

LUCILLE CLIFTON

DAUGHTERS

woman who shines at the head
of my grandmother's bed,
brilliant woman, i like to think
you whispered into her ear
instructions. i like to think
you are the oddness in us,
you are the arrow
that pierced our plain skin
and made us fancy women;
my wild witch gran, my magic mama,
and even these gaudy girls.
i like to think you gave us
extraordinary power and to
protect us, you became the name
we were cautioned to forget.
it is enough,
you must have murmured,
to remember that i was
and that you are. woman, i am
lucille, which stands for light,
daughter of thelma, daughter
of georgia, daughter of
dazzling you.

RAINY DAWN ORTIZ

Every Day It Is Always There

Every day it is always there
Whether in mind or body
Whether I want it to be or not—
Sometimes it's like being haunted
By a constant presence
Of sometimes happiness
Sometimes anger—
But it is always filled with love.
That love is my protector.
That love is my mother.

JOY HARJO

RAINY DAWN

I can still close my eyes and open them four floors up looking south
    and west
from the hospital, the approximate direction of Acoma, and farther
    on to the
roofs of the houses of the gods who have learned there are no
    endings, only
beginnings. That day so hot, heat danced in waves off bright car
    tops, we both
stood poised at that door from the east, listened for a long time to
    the sound
of our grandmothers' voices, the brushing wind of sacred wings,
    the rattle of
raindrops in dry gourds. I had to participate in the dreaming of you
    into memory—
cupped your head in the bowl of my body as ancestors lined up to
    give you
a name made of their dreams cast once more into this stew of
    precious spirit
and flesh. And let you go, as I am letting you go once more in this
    ceremony
of the living. And when you were born I held you wet and
    unfolding,
like a butterfly newly born from the chrysalis of my body. And
    breathed
with you as you breathed your first breath. Then was your
    promise to
take it on like the rest of us, this immense journey, for love, for rain.

GLORIA VANDO

GROWING INTO LILAC

Three women in lilac saris, their scarves
uncurling in the cool afternoon breeze,
carry their children in their arms beneath
a canopy of jacaranda trees,

their lavender blossoms scribbling love notes
on the clear blue sky. I slow down my car
to savor this moment of intense spring—
and find myself back in Playa del Mar

with my friend Meryl, who, after her son
died, painted her daughter's bedroom in swirls
of lilac, dressed her bed with a lilac
spread and, as if to shield her from the world's

sorrows, hung heavy lilac drapes across
her window. I found the color morose—
not quite blue, not quite rose—a muted
display of Meryl's unutterable loss.

I was a new mother, then, both too old
and too young for the subtleties of lilac.
Now, my daughter grown and gone, the color
feels right—fits me like an embryonic sac.

TEREZE GLÜCK

YELLOW LIGHT

We lay by the water's edge, the blue and green drift of sea creeping towards us. My mother wore a bathing suit the colour of an orange. Later I knew it for what it was, a risky colour, a young colour, and even then I suspected. My mother had a connection to colour, was how she put it, and thought that even the blue of the water was hers. She thought she could do anything she wanted: put a whole body of colours together, and she liked to do just that. In hot weather she favoured pastels. I like pale colours, she said, bleached colours. Colours called—she said them aloud to me—peach, aqua, shell, mint, seafoam, banana. Banana yellow is a very particular shade of yellow, she told me. A very pale yellow.

We were in Mexico, lying on the sand beach, where men walked barefoot along the dark wet sand by the water's edge, selling their wares. My mother bought me a silver ring with a turquoise in the centre, and three bracelets for herself. Behind us was the curved arc of hotels, their gardens of bougainvillea, hibiscus, jacaranda. My mother, who loved the names of things, told me these.

"I'm feeling better," she said. "I'm recovering."

She had come here to recover, I wasn't sure from what but I had an idea. Recovery meant sun. She said the sun was a restorative. Already I knew her ways: how she would lie there, grains of sand sticking to her shining body. The sun reflected in her flat parts: her thighs, her chest, sometimes the flat of her cheek. Lying beside her I thought of her body as terrain, and these were the plains, the prairies, that glistened in the sun. It wasn't the suntan she was after; I'd overheard her explaining that to friends one summer at our house on the lake. It was the sensation, the burning itself. She said it bleached her brain and that was all to the good.

I knew if I lay there beside her long enough she would tell me something. I always knew when she was telling me things that were marginal, that she probably shouldn't be telling me. Usually it was about men, or love, or my father, but it might be her ideas about life: things she took for wisdom and thought she could hand on to me. At last she had a captive audience. She'd start in. "That Gordon," she says. "He broke my heart." I put my hands to my ears. "Don't tell me," I say; "I'm your child." Don't tell me, I'd say, even then, at seven, eight, nine.

"Oh, my poor Poppy!" she said, and laughed. "Poor old thing!" She had as many nicknames for me as she had colours or daydreams. She didn't have plans but she had plenty of daydreams. She scorned plans and I often would hear her, usually driving in the car with one of her friends and us, the children, in the back seat, complain of this or that person and his plans. "As if they had any control!" she said, and from the back seat I remember the shake of her head, the flyaway hair. People with plans were one of her complaints. She said they reproached her. "Sometimes I wish I could clear everybody off the planet," she said. "But then who'd drive," I said; because she didn't know how to drive and we relied on other people to get around. In the city it didn't matter, we walked or took taxis; but elsewhere we either went with friends or we didn't go.

Here's the sun.

So long as there's sun, my mother says, I make no demands of the universe.

Meanwhile I'm burning. My mother rubs lotion on my body, clears the hair away from my face and with her finger beneath my chin, arches my head upwards. "You have your father's skin," she says. "English skin." My father is, in addition to being English, tall, pale and bony. She says my body is his as well and that I walk just like him.

With her finger she's rubbing lotion on my cheeks, my nose. "Promise me something," she says.

"I promise," I say.

"But you don't know what yet!" she says.

"I promise anyway."

"Promise you'll never leave me," she says.

I was a knowing child. I watch her, swear I can see her skin mixing its colours, agitating and darkening before my very eyes, alive with cells. "Remember," I say, full of genius so vivid I can feel it jump in my skin—"Remember when I was inside your body?"

She turns her face toward me, glistening with amber oil. "Oh Poppy!" she says, clapping her hands, smiling her smile. "I remember!"

Sometimes I swear too that I do remember: dark, a mire as thick and smooth as velvet, the heartbeat. My mother often repeated a story to me, one which I myself recall. At three or four how I said to her: where did I used to be? and she said: inside me. I was silent a moment, and then said: I'm sorry I had to be born because now I have to be outside.

I will say this for myself: I always knew what my mother wanted, and I gave it to her.

Clouds are coming; she'll mind.

I steel myself, my heart, willing them away. She'll ignore them a while, strain towards cheer. "I have a theory," she says. "I fool the sun: When it's cloudy I lie out, grease myself up, just as if the sun were out. And the sun sees me, and it thinks—oh—I must be out, people are lying in me!"

She thought she could will anything: the sun to come out, the clouds to disperse, a man to love her.

In this at least she was right: she willed me. She said so. "Here you are," she'd say. "—here you are; I did it! I made you be here!"

"Come on, sun!" my mother said.

She told me how she had travelled along the coast of Portugal when she was young, how she and a friend had flung themselves onto the sand, even though it was April and still cool, and had flung their arms out to the side and said, "Bake me, sol!"

181

The sky was spotty anyway, even with her tricks: part cloud, holes in the clouds and moments of sun. I could see her thinking, how that the clouds were out and there was no direct heat from the sun to ward off thought. "About these men," she said. "I don't know what it is I do wrong. What is it I do wrong?"

In a few minutes the sun was out again and my mother said she had no business telling me half the things she did, but that was the way she was, and that was how it was going to be.

My mother, in Mexico, at family reunions in Amagansett, by the green lake in Connecticut, keeps watch for a cloudless sky. "I want azure," she says. "I want turquoise."

"Little peach," she says to me. "Little bear. It's good to have so many names. The Chinese have a saying: a well-loved child has many names. I don't know where I heard it. Maybe I made it up. But it's true."

We look into each other's eyes. Her pupils in the bright sun are tiny. Her eyes are a nameless colour, khaki, she says, the colour of army tanks. "'Oh, your eyes are the colour of army tanks!'" she mocks.

She sighs, her eyes looking up now, a watchful hunter, hunting for light. When it comes, unequivocal, that untarnished sun, it refracts off the shine of her skin, encasing me in a double warmth: its own, and hers.

Ever since I was a child, she says, this is what I've hankered after. My first broken heart. My father took me to Bermuda where I nursed my broken heart in the sun. I burned myself rightly there. We rented a boat with white sails and I lay on the bow, where the wind and sun both got me. In the morning my face was as puffed up as a melon and they had to give me pills to bring it down. Who could recollect a heart, broken or otherwise, under such a scorch, such searing?

My mother told me amazing things. There is a perfume, she said,

182

by which I mean odour, not one you wear, which belongs with this landscape, although it is not here. She stopped then. With me at least she could be mysterious. But I did not care to prompt her. "The fragrance I have in mind," she said, "is oranges. I will tell you about the first time I smelled orange trees in bloom. It was in Seville, in the south of Spain." I knew the word, Spain, and that it was a country, but that was all.

She told me that in this city, Seville, the streets were made of cobblestone, and you could hear the horses' hooves on the cobbled roads, that their hooves echoed on the stone. "I remember all that," she said, "but primarily it was a place you could smell—overpowering, that perfume, pungent, stifling—I mean the smell of oranges."

"Oranges" I repeat, trying to imagine their smell. "The colour," I say, "of your bathing suit."

She props herself up on an elbow, I can see where the white skin meets, turns, brown. She's smiling at me. "You are a brilliant child," she says. "You are an ingenious person. And that's what I think."

She dives into the turquoise water and I watch her orange bathing suit and her shining skin send off light. I watch her the way a child watches its mother. She kicks up water like a fish, one of those flying kinds of fish, and then she turns and looks at me and I look right back. She walks toward me through the water and I stand there and let her. The light is in her eyes but I can see her fine.

And so it goes, each of us trying to surprise the other. The day proceeds and soon the sky begins to darken, until in the argument of light, the brilliant yellow concedes to gray. That day, my mother had so much sun on her I thought she'd become sun, herself. That day, and every day before it, and after, we seduced one another, until, by evening, in the clearer light of dusk, we were back together again, one body, one skin.

SONIA SANCHEZ

DEAR MAMA

It is Christmas Eve and the year is passing away with calloused feet. My father, your son, and I decorate the night with words. Sit ceremoniously in human song. Watch our blue sapphire words eclipse the night. We have come to this simplicity from afar.

He stirs, pulls from his pocket a faded picture of you. Black-woman. Sitting in frigid peace. All of your biography preserved in your face. And my eyes draw up short as he says, "her name was Elizabeth but we used to call her Lizzie." And I hold your picture in my hands. But I know your name by heart. It's Mama. I hold you in my hands and let time pass over my face: "Let my baby be. She ain't like the others. She rough. She'll stumble on gentleness later on."

Ah Mama. Gentleness ain't never been no stranger to my genes. But I did like the roughness of running and swallowing the wind, diving in rivers I could barely swim, jumping from second story windows into a saving backyard bush. I did love you for loving me so hard until I slid inside your veins and sailed your blood to an uncrucified shore.

And I remember Saturday afternoons at our house. The old sister deaconesses sitting in sacred pain. Black cadavers burning with lost aromas. And I crawled behind the couch and listened to breaths I had never breathed. Tasted their enormous martyrdom. Lives spent on so many things. Heard their laughter at Sister Smith's latest performance in church—her purse sailing toward Brother Thomas's head again. And I hugged the laughter round my knees. Draped it round my shoulder like a Spanish shawl.

And history began once again. I received it and let it circulate in my blood. I learned on those Saturday afternoons about women rooted in themselves, raising themselves in dark America, discharging their pain without ever stopping. I learned about women fighting men back when they hit them: "Don't never let no mens hit you mo than once girl." I learned about "womens waking up they mens" in the night with pans of hot grease and the compromises reached after the smell of hot grease had penetrated their sleepy brains. I learned about loose women walking their abandoned walk down front in church, crossing their legs instead of their hands to God. And I crept into my eyes. Along with my daydreams of being woman. Adult. Powerful. Loving. Like them. Allowing nobody to rule me if I didn't want to be.

And when they left. When those old bodies had gathered up their sovereign smells. After they had kissed and packed up beans snapped and cakes cooked and laughter bagged. After they had called out their last goodbyes, I crawled out of my place. Surveyed the room. Then walked over to the couch where some had sat for hours and bent my head and smelled their evening smells. I screamed out loud, "Oooweeee! Ain't that stinky!" and I laughed laughter from a thousand corridors. And you turned Mama, closed the door, chased me round the room until I crawled into a corner where your large body could not reach me. But your laughter pierced the little alcove where I sat laughing at the night. And your humming sprinkled my small space. Your humming about your Jesus and how one day he was gonna take you home…

Because you died when I was six Mama, I never laughed like that again. Because you died without warning Mama, my sister and I moved from family to stepmother to friend of the family. I never felt your warmth again.

But I knew corners and alcoves and closets where I was pushed when some mad woman went out of control. Where I sat for days while some woman raved in rhymes about unwanted children. And work. And not enough money. Or love. And I sat out my childhood with stutters and poems gathering in my head like some winter storm. And the poems erased the stutters and pain. And the words loved me and I loved them in return.

My first real poem was about you Mama and death. My first real poem recited an alphabet of spit splattering a white bus driver's face after he tried to push cousin Lucille off a bus and she left

Birmingham under the cover of darkness. Forever. My first real poem was about your Charleswhite arms hold me up against death.

My life flows from you Mama. My style comes from a long line of Louises who picked me up in the night to keep me from wetting the bed. A long line of Sarahs who fed me and my sister and fourteen other children from watery soup and beans and a lot of imagination. A long line of Lizzies who made me understand love. Sharing. Holding a child up to the stars. Holding your tribe in a grip of love. A long line of Black people holding each other up against silence.

I still hear your humming Mama. The color of your song calls me home. The color of your words saying, "Let her be. She got a right to be different. She gonna stumble on herself one of these days. Just let the child be."

And I be, Mama.

NELLY SACHS

WE MOTHERS

We mothers,
we gather seed of desire
from oceanic night,
we are gatherers
of scattered goods.

We mothers,
pacing dreamily
with the constellations,
the floods
of past and future,
leave us alone
with our birth
like an island…

We who impel sand to love and bring
a mirroring world to the stars—

We mothers,
who rock in the cradles
the shadowy memories
of creation's day—
the to and fro of each breath
is the melody of our love song.

We mothers
rock into the heart of the world
the melody of peace.

Acknowledgments & Permissions

Without Kathryn Stripling Byer's inspiration and loyalty to the project, this volume would not have taken flight. The contributors have demonstrated remarkable patience in addition to their creativity. Dr. Julia Demmin has offered encouragement and editorial wisdom over the years.

Several talented young writers have provided research assistance in the development of this project. These have included James "Bucky" Carter, Laura Hoffer, Casie Fedukovich and Jessie Janeshek, graduate students in creative writing or writing and rhetoric at the University of Tennessee. Jessie Janeshek has helped to shape the final version of the manuscript. The Graduate Office of the English Department has supported these research assistantships for *The Movable Nest*. While a Master of Fine Arts student at New York University, Lauren McCollum helped to edit an early version of this manuscript. Jennie Devenski Currin, a Knoxville educator now teaching in Louisville, also provided editorial assistance.

Editor Ben Furnish at BkMk Press offered steady encouragement. Holly Carver, editor at the University of Iowa Press, provided valuable feedback in the early stages of this manuscript. Gloria Vando Hickok welcomed the project on board and secured grants for its publication.

Funding for this anthology has been provided by the Kansas Arts Commission, the Missouri Arts Council, and the Miller-Mellor Association. The Hodges Fund of the English Department and the Humanities Initiative of the Office of Research at the University of Tennessee provided generous book subventions. Dr. John Zomchick, Head of the English Department, has guided these grants to fruition. His support of faculty research and publication at the University of Tennessee has been invaluable.

The editors are deeply grateful.

BIOGRAPHICAL NOTES

Betty Adcock is the author of five books of poetry from Louisiana State University Press, most recently *Intervale: New and Selected Poems*, which was co-winner of the 2003 Poets' Prize. Her sixth book, *Slantwise*, is forthcoming from Louisiana State University Press in the spring of 2008. She has held numerous fellowships, including a Guggenheim Fellowship in Poetry from 2002-2003.

Deedee Agee is working on a collection of autobiographical stories set in Greenwich Village in the 1950s and '60s. She has taught writing privately and in New York area colleges, and has also worked as a waitress, house painter, reproductive counselor, chef, and software trainer at the United Nations.

Lauren K. Alleyne, a native of Trinidad and Tobago, received her Master of Fine Arts degree in Creative Writing from Cornell University. Her work has been awarded the 2003 *Atlantic Monthly* Student Poetry Prize and has been published in several journals, including *Black Arts Quarterly*. She is the Writing Center Coordinator at Weill Cornell Medical College in Qatar, and a Cave Canem Fellow.

Maggie Anderson is the author of four books of poems, most recently *Windfall: New and Selected Poems* (2000). She is the co-editor, with David Hassler, of *After the Bell: Contemporary American Prose about School* and the editor of *Hill Daughter: New and Selected Poems of Louise McNeill*. She directs the Wick Poetry Center and edits the Wick Poetry Series of the Kent State University Press.

Corinna Lynette Byer, a native of Cullowhee, North Carolina, is a graduate student in the South Asian Studies Department at the University of Texas-Austin. She received her B.A. from the University of Chicago. Her scholarly work has been published in *The Annual of Urdu Studies*, and her poetry in *Now and Then*, *The North Carolina Writers Network Newsletter*, and *Award Winning Poems* (North Carolina Poetry Society).

Kathryn Stripling Byer's fifth poetry collection is *Coming to Rest* (LSU Press, 2006). Her work has appeared in journals ranging from *The Atlantic Monthly* to *Appalachian Heritage* and has received numerous literary and academic honors from the Academy of American Poets, National Endowment for the Arts, Fellowship of Southern Writers, and others. She was appointed Poet Laureate of North Carolina in 2005.

Jeanette Cabanis-Brewin, a business writer and editor, is the 2007 winner of the Longleaf Press Chapbook Award for her chapbook, *Patriate*. Her poetry has been published in *The Nomad, Atlanta Review*, and *Appalachian Heritage*, and in the anthologies *Tree Magic* (SunShine Press, 2004), *The Gift of Experience* (Atlanta Review, 2005), and *Immigration, Emigration, Diversity* (Chapel Hill Press, 2005).

Andrée Chedid has written three volumes of short stories, two collections of plays, three short prose works, and eleven novels. She is the recipient of the highest award of the Académie Mallarmé for poetry (1976); Grand Prix de la Poésie de la Société des Gens de Lettres; Prix Albert Camus for the novel (1996); and Grand Prix Paul Morand (2001) for her entire opus. Born in Cairo, Egypt, of Lebanese and Syrian descent, she lives in Paris.

Marilyn Chin's latest book is *Rhapsody in Plain Yellow*. She has won grants from the NEA, the Stegner Fellowship, the PEN/Josephine Miles Award, a Fulbright Fellowship to Taiwan, and four Pushcarts. Her poems are in *The Norton Anthology of Modern Poetry, The Oxford Anthology of Modern American Poetry, Unsettling America,* and *The Best American Poetry of 1996*. She co-directs the MFA program at San Diego State University.

Lucille Clifton won the 2007 Ruth Lilly Poetry Prize and was a finalist for the Pulitzer Prize and the National Book Award. Her work includes collections of poetry, children's books, and an autobiographical prose work. Her newest books are *Blessing the Boats: New and Selected Poems* and *Mercy*. Poet Laureate of Maryland from 1975-1985, she was Distinguished Professor of the Humanities at St. Mary's College of Maryland until 2005.

Judy Pfau Cochran is Professor of French at Denison University, where she teaches French language and literature and edits *Collage*. She translated two bilingual editions of poetry by Andrée Chedid: *Territories of Breath / Territoires du souffle: Bilingual Translation* and *Selected Poems of Andrée Chedid*. With Renée Linkhorn, she edited the bilingual volume *Belgian Women Poets: An Anthology*.

Moira Crone is the author of four books of fiction, most recently the novel in stories, *What Gets Into Us* (University of Mississippi Press 2006). On five occasions, her short stories won inclusion in *New Stories from the South: The Year's Best*. She has received grants from the NEA, the NEH, and the Bunting Institute at Harvard/Radcliffe. She has been published in *The New Yorker, Mademoiselle*, and *TriQuarterly*.

Rita Dove served as Poet Laureate of the United States and Consultant to the Library of Congress from 1993-1995 and is currently Poet Laureate of the Commonwealth of Virginia, where she is Professor of English at the University of Virginia in Charlottesville. She received the 1987 Pulitzer Prize in poetry. Her new collection is *American Smooth* (W.W. Norton).

193

Janice Eidus, novelist, short story writer, and essayist, has twice won the O. Henry Prize, as well as a Redbook Prize and a Pushcart Prize. Her books include the story collections, *The Celibacy Club* and *Vito Loves Geraldine*; the novels, *Urban Bliss* and *Faithful Rebecca;* and *It's Only Rock And Roll: An Anthology of Rock And Roll Short Stories*, which she co-edited. Her new novel is *The War of the Rosens*.

Alice Friman's new poetry book is *The Book of the Rotten Daughter* (BkMk Press). Her poems appear in *Poetry, Boulevard, The Georgia Review,* and others. She has won three prizes from the Poetry Society of America and in 2001 was named to the Georgia Poetry Circuit. Professor Emerita at the University of Indianapolis, she is now Poet-in-Residence at Georgia College & State University.

Diane Gilliam's books include: *Kettle Bottom, One of Everything*, and *Recipe for Blackberry Cake* (chapbook). In 2003 she received an Ohio Arts Council Individual Artist Fellowship. In 2005 she won the Ohioana Library Association Book of the Year Award for *Kettle Bottom,*which also won a Pushcart Prize and was an American Booksellers Association Book Sense Pick for the Top Ten Poetry Books of 2005.

Tereze Glück is a graduate of Vassar College. Her collection of stories *May You Live in Interesting Times* won the 1995 Iowa Short Fiction Award. She has received a grant from the National Endowment for the Arts and has been a fellow at the Virginia Center for the Creative Arts, Ragdale, and Ucross. Her work has been published in the *North American Review*, *Antioch Review,* and the *Gettysburg Review*.

Sarah Gorham's collections of poetry are *The Cure, The Tension Zone*, and *Don't Go Back to Sleep*. Her poems and essays have appeared in *American Poetry Review, Southern Review, Five Points, Gettysburg Review, Prairie Schooner, Best American Poetry 2006*, and *Poets and Writers*. She is President and Editor-in-Chief of Sarabande Books, an independent literary press she founded with Jeffrey Skinner in 1994.

Joy Harjo is a poet, performer, writer, and musician, and member of the Mvskoke/Creek Nation in Oklahoma. *How We Became Human, New and Selected Poems* is her most recent collection. Her albums include *Letter from the End of the 20th Century* and *Native Joy for Real*. She has performed internationally and is currently the Joseph M. Russo endowed professor in Creative Writing at the University of New Mexico.

Brenda Hillman teaches at St. Mary's College in California, where she is the Olivia Fillipi Professor of English and Drama. She is the author of several collections of poetry, including *Coffee 3 AM*, *White Dress*, *Fortress*, *Death Tractates*, *Bright Existence*, *Loose Sugar*, *Cascadia*, and *Pieces of Air in the Epic*, and the co-editor of *The Grand Permission: New Writings on Poetics and Motherhood*.

Colette Inez has written nine poetry collections, most recently *Spinoza Doesn't Come Here Anymore* (Melville House Books). Widely anthologized, she has received numerous fellowships and prizes (Guggenheim and Rockefeller Foundations, National Endowment for the Arts, Pushcart). She is on the faculty of Columbia University's Undergraduate Writing Program. Her memoir, *The Secret of M. Dulong*, was published in 2005 by the University of Wisconsin Press.

Jessie L. Janeshek is a doctoral student in English at the University of Tennessee, working on a poetry collection. She holds a Master of Fine Arts in poetry from Emerson College. Her poems have appeared in *The Sow's Ear Poetry Review, Washington Square, Passages North, EvaMag, New Millennium Writings, Caduceus,* and *Review Americana.*

Allison Joseph lives, writes, and teaches in Carbondale, Illinois, where she's on the creative writing faculty at Southern Illinois University. Her books of poems include *Worldly Pleasures* (Word Press, 2004), *What Keeps Us Here* (Ampersand Press), *In Every Seam* (University of Pittsburgh Press), and *Imitation of Life* (Carnegie Mellon University Press).

Marilyn Kallet is the author of fourteen books, including *Circe, After Hours,* poetry (BkMk Press, 2005) and *Last Love Poems of Paul Eluard,* translations (Black Widow Press, 2006). She co-edited *Sleeping With One Eye Open: Women Writers and the Art of Survival.* She holds a Lindsay Young Professorship in English at the University of Tennessee, where she directed the creative writing program from 1986-2003.

Meg Kearney's first collection of poetry is *An Unkindness of Ravens* (2001). Four Way Books will publish *Home By Now* in 2009. *The Secret of Me* (2005) is her novel in verse for teens. Her poetry has appeared in *Poetry, Agni,* and *Ploughshares.* She is director of the Solstice Low-Residency Master of Fine Arts in Creative Writing Program at Pine Manor College in Chestnut Hill, Massachusetts.

Jamaica Kincaid was born on the island of Antigua, and her works draw primarily from her Caribbean childhood. In 1978, her fiction was published in *The New Yorker,* and later became part of her book, *At the Bottom of the River* (1983). Her first novel, *Annie John,* followed in 1985. Other writings include *Lucy, The Autobiography of My Mother, My Garden,* and *Among Flowers: A Walk in the Himalayas.*

Renée Linkhorn, born in Liège, Belgium, is Professor Emerita of French at Youngstown State University and is a translator and editor of the works of French-speaking writers. Her publications include *The Prose and Poetry of Andrée Chedid* (Summa Publications, 1990), *La Belgique telle qu'elle s'écrit* (Peter Lang, 1995) and *Belgian Women Poets: An Anthology* (Peter Lang, 2000), co-authored with Judy Cochran. She writes bilingual poetry under the pen name Renée Laurentine.

195

Linda Parsons Marion is the poetry editor of *Now & Then* magazine and the author of *Home Fires.* Her poems have appeared in *The Georgia Review, Shenandoah, Iowa Review, Prairie Schooner, Nimrod, Negative Capability, Cornbread Nation 2, and CALYX,* among others. She has received two literary fellowships from the Tennessee Arts Commission.

Libby Martinez was born and raised in El Paso, Texas, on the U.S./ Mexico border and is a graduate of the University of Texas at Austin and Stanford Law School. After a decade of working in the Texas political and business development arena, she has embarked on a second career, seeking to enhance people's aesthetic interaction with their world through both writing and design.

Rebecca McClanahan most recent books are *Deep Light: New and Selected Poems 1987-2007* (Iris Press) and *The Riddle Song and Other Rememberings*, which won the 2005 Glasgow Award for nonfiction. Her work is in *The Best American Essays*, the Pushcart anthology, and *The Best American Poetry* series. She teaches in the low-residency MFA program of Queens University in Charlotte and the Kenyon Review Writers Workshop.

Lauren McCollum's work has appeared in *Poetry, Willard & Maple*, and *New Millennium Writings*. She earned her undergraduate degree in English at Princeton University and her Master of Fine Arts in poetry at New York University

Pat Mora latest collection is *Adobe Odes* (2006, University of Arizona Press). An author of poetry, nonfiction, and more than 30 children's books, she received an Honorary Doctorate in Letters from Buffalo State College (SUNY) in 2006. She is the founder of the family literacy initiative *El día de los niños/ El día de los libros*, Children's Day/Book Day at the American Library Association.

Sharon Olds is the author of eight books of poetry, most recently *Strike Sparks: Selected Poems*, 1980-2002 (2004). Her book, *The Father,* was shortlisted for the T. S. Eliot Prize in 1994, and *The Unswept Room* was a nominee for the National Book Award in 2002. Other honors include an Academy Fellowship from the Academy of American Poets in 2002. She was New York State Poet Laureate from 1998–2000 and is Professor of English and Creative Writing at New York University.

Rainy Dawn Ortiz is an Acoma Pueblo tribal member, born of the Myskoke people in Albuquerque, New Mexico. Her first poems were published in a Tucson, Arizona, Teenage Parent Program student publication (1990). She writes poetry inspired by her family and has performed her work at the University of Rochester, New York, and the University of New Mexico at Gallup. She is working on a series of laundromat stories.

Alicia Ostriker, twice a finalist for the National Book Award, has published eleven volumes of poetry, including *No Heaven* (2005). Her most recent prose work is *For the Love of God: the Bible as an Open Book.* Her poetry has appeared in *The New Yorker, American Poetry Review, The Atlantic,* and *Ontario Review.* She teaches in the low-residency Poetry Master of Fine Arts program of New England College.

Linda Pastan's twelfth book of poems, *Queen of a Rainy Country,* was published by Norton in October of 2006. She has twice been a finalist for The National Book Award, and in 2003 she received the Ruth Lilly Poetry Prize. She served as Poet Laureate of Maryland from 1991-1995.

Rochelle Ratner's books include two novels and seventeen poetry books, most recently *Leads: A poem, memoir, journal* (Otoliths, 2007). An anthology she edited, *Bearing Life: Women's Writings on Childlessness,* was published in January 2000 by The Feminist Press. A former Executive Editor and current Associate Editor for *American Book Review,* she reviews regularly for *Library Journal.*

Hilda Raz's books include *Divine Honors* and *Trans* (Wesleyan, 2001) and most recently *What Becomes You,* essays with Aaron Raz Link, (University of Nebraska Press, 2007). She is the Luschei Endowed Editor of *Prairie Schooner* and a Professor of English and Women's & Gender Studies at University of Nebraska-Lincoln.

Paulette Roeske's five books include *Divine Attention,* winner of the Carl Sandburg Book Award for Poetry; and *Bridge of Sighs,* winner of the Three Oaks Prize for Fiction. She received an Illinois Arts Council fellowship and the Chester H. Jones National Poetry Competition Prize. Her work has appeared in *Poetry, The Georgia Review,* and *Glimmer Train.* She was a visiting poet at Harlaxton College and at Christ Church College in England.

Nelly Sachs, co-winner of the 1966 Nobel Prize for Literature, was born in Berlin in 1891. Her first volume of poetry, *In the Dwellings of Death* (1946), was followed by *O the Chimneys,* and others. Reflecting her continuing struggle to pay homage to the unique anguish of the Jews during the Holocaust, her work builds a vision of universal human suffering that might lead to reconciliation, if not redemption. She died in Sweden in 1970.

Sonia Sanchez is the author of sixteen books, most recently, *Shake Loose My Skin* (Beacon Press, 1999). She has edited *We Be Word Sorcerers: 25 Stories by Black Americans* and *360° of Blackness Coming at You.* A recipient of a National Endowment for the Arts award, she also won the American Book Award, a Pew Fellowship in the Arts, and a Langston Hughes Poetry Award. The first Presidential Fellow at Temple University, she held the Laura Carnell Chair in English.

Pamela Schoenewaldt lives in Knoxville, where she teaches writing at the University of Tennessee and has been the library's Writer in Residence. Her fiction has appeared in *Belletrist Review, New Letters, Crescent Review, Literal Latté, Paris Transcontinental, Potomac Review, Square Lake, The Sun*, and *Women's Words*. She has won the Chekhov Prize, the Leslie Garrett Prize, and Literal Latté's Fiction Award.

Barbara Selfridge is the author of *Serious Kissing*, a collection of stories published by Glad Day Books. Her work has been honored with fellowships from Poets & Writers, the National Endowment for the Arts, the Fine Arts Work Center in Provincetown, and other artist residencies. She is currently working on stories about life with her older developmentally disabled sister.

Nonie Selfridge Sparks (1925-2001) was a programmer on SWAC, the early 1950's computer located at UCLA.

Katherine Smith's work has appeared or is forthcoming in a number of journals and reviews, among them *Fiction International, Poetry, The Southern Review, Appalachian Heritage, Atlanta Review* and *The Louisville Review*. Her first book, *Argument by Design*, won the Washington Writers' Publishing House Poetry Prize and appeared in 2003. She teaches at Montgomery College in Germantown, Maryland.

Gloria Vando's work has appeared in many magazines, anthologies, and in the 2006 Grammy-nominated *Poetry on Record: 98 Poets Read Their Work 1888-2006*. Her latest book, *Shadows and Supposes* (Arte Público Press), won the Poetry Society of America's Di Castagnola Award and the Latino Literary Hall of Fame's Poetry Book Award. She publishes Helicon Nine Editions and is co-founder of The Writers Place in Kansas City.

Ingrid Wendt has written four books of poetry, a chapbook, and the teaching guide, *Starting with Little Things*. She has taught in the Master of Fine Arts program of Antioch University in Los Angeles, at teacher-training institutes throughout the United .States., and in hundreds of public school classrooms. Honors include the Carolyn Kizer Award, the D.H. Lawrence Award, and three Fulbright professorships to Germany.

J. Patrice Whetsell has been an Artist-in-Residence at the Ragdale Foundation, the Headlands Center for the Arts, and the Vermont Studio Center. Her stories have appeared in *Glimmer Train, Kalliope*, and the anthology *Mother Knows: 24 Tales of Motherhood (2004)*. She lives in North Carolina where she divides her time between graduate studies at UNC Chapel Hill, caring for two rabbits, and working on her first novel.

Dede Wilson is the author of three books of poems, *Glass,* published as a finalist in the Persephone Press Competition, *Sea of Small Fears*, winner of the Main Street Rag Chapbook Competition, and *One Nightstand*. Her poems have appeared in *Carolina Quarterly, Spoon River Poetry Review, Cream City, Flyway, Asheville Poetry Review, The Lyric,* and *Light.*

Lillian Elaine Wilson (Friman) graduated from Purdue University with a B.A. in photography and works for the J. Paul Getty Museum. Her portrait of actor/photographer Leonard Nimoy was published full page in the book *TV Land Legends* along with photographs by Herb Ritts and Annie Leibovitz. In April 2007, her series, "Life Stop 217," was exhibited at Farmani Gallery in Los Angeles.

Cecilia Woloch is the author of *Sacrifice; Tsigan: The Gypsy Poem*; and *Late*, for which she was named Georgia Author of the Year in Poetry for 2004. Her chapbook, *Narcissus*, won the Snowbound Prize from Tupelo Press and will be published in 2007. She teaches in the Master of Fine Arts Program at Western Connecticut State University and undergraduate creative writing at the University of Southern California.

Barbara Zimmermann (Bogue) teaches fiction writing and directs the yearly Creative Writing in the Community project at Ball State University. She is the author of *James Lee Burke and the Soul of Dave Robicheaux: A Critical Study of the Crime Fiction Series.* Her fiction, poetry, and literary nonfiction have appeared in *New Millennium Writings, Pleiades,* and *Kaleidoscope.*

199

INDEX